THIS BOOK INCLUDES

BOOK 1: 10 (FIRST PAGE)

609 Letter Template And Credit Repair:

A Comprehensive Beginner's Guide To Your Score
Secrets And Credit Repair.Including How To Write
A 609 Letter And Templates.

BOOK 2: 190 (FIRST PAGE)

Credit Score Secret:

A Complete Beginner's Guide On How To Repair
Your Credit, Improve Your Score, And Boost
Your Business. Including How To Write
A 609 Dispute Letter.

609 LETTER TEMPLATE AND CREDIT REPAIR:

A Comprehensive Beginner's Guide To Your Score Secrets And Credit Repair. Including How To Write A 609 Letter And Templates.

Scott Moss

Table Of Contents

Introduction

A credit score is simply a rank of your creditworthiness with a goal number. In the past, if you need credit you would have to go into the bank, and if you had a decent remaining in the network, or if the advance official had a positive sentiment about you, you could get an advance. However, there is a blemish in that framework; anyone can have bad credit despite how very much regarded they are. Along these lines, by computing the impact of various factors on your capacity to reimburse, the credit offices concocted a way that tries to treat everyone decently.

The problems that come with not having a good credit rating can be dangerous. However, you do not have to worry about having a bad rating for too long if you use the right efforts to get the best credit rating you can earn. Knowing what you are getting out of your cards and how they work is critical to your success regarding covering those cards and keeping them from costing more to use than what you can afford.

Learning about credit and finance can be an intimidating task. I believe one should seek to understand anything they choose to participate in. We don't choose when it comes to credit, so why not have the knowledge and understanding of it regardless of any trade or career you are in or will pursue? Credit can always be used as a leverage tool no matter how much money you have or make. Pay attention to how wealthy people secure mortgages to purchase their property and pay interest while still building equity.

Still, to truly live a happy life, you need to make sure that you are financially stable. This is done by saving money, getting your credit in good shape, and eliminating debt. Credit repair is a great solution for those needing to fix their bad credit. Understanding how it works can be a bit tough, so the goal here is to provide good information accessible to everyone and viable solutions for people with bad credit.

This book contains proven steps and strategies for saving money and getting yourself in better financial shape. It can help you identify what you can do to get a better credit rating for your life. You will read about many things related to your credit, including what goes into your rating. You can figure out what you can do to improve your credit rating based on what can go into that rating and how it can make a real difference in your life. This book also provides actionable steps and strategies to improve your credit score quickly and take full control of your financial life.

The details on what you can do to manage your credit are varied. You can use many sensible strategies for managing your credit while using the right decisions. You can also get in touch with credit reporting bureaus to fix any problems you have on your report. The best part is that all these details are ones that you can utilize yourself. You might not have to spend more money than what you are trying to cover on your credit profile. That is, you don't have to contact some outside credit repair group that would not do much of anything to help you. Most importantly, you will not have to worry about such a credit repair group ripping you off with the false belief that you could get some real credit help from that entity.

Of course, sometimes you might be working well on managing your credit, but it could suddenly take a massive hit if your identity is stolen. This guide also includes details on how you can repair your credit rating if you become a victim of identity theft. This is a legitimate problem that has become very common throughout the world. Hence, you need to look for ways to resolve your credit-related issues following a case where you have been victimized by identity theft.

The details you will come across in this guide will help you resolve the many problems you might come across when it comes to your credit rating. Be sure to see what this guide has to offer to find that it is not overly difficult for you to get the most out of improving your credit.

CHAPTER 1:

Basics of Credit Repair

HOW CREDIT REPAIR WORKS

Although various organizations guarantee they can tidy up bad credit reports, amending incorrect data that may show up on layaway reports requires some serious energy and exertion. An outsider can't expel the subtleties referred to credit revealing offices. Or maybe the subtleties, whenever distorted or erroneous, can be questioned.

Credit repair organizations may research such data; however, the individual is also evaluating the report. People are qualified with the expectation of complimentary credit reports at regular intervals from credit revealing offices, just as when an unfavorable move is made against them. For example, being turned down regarding credit dependent on data in the report.

Debates might be documented when deficient or mistaken data shows up on their credit reports. Besides remedying such data, or getting false exchanges on one's credit, modifying and fixing credit can lay even more intensely on layaway utilization and credit movement.

The payment history of the individual can be a critical factor in their credit standing. Finding a way to ensure installments are modern or improving the installment plan for exceptional credits can influence their financial assessment. Moreover, the measure of credit utilized by the individual can likewise assume a job. For example, suppose an individual is effectively utilizing huge bits of the credit accessible to them. In that case, regardless of whether they are keeping up the least installments on schedule, the size of the obligation they are conveying can contrarily influence their credit score. The issue is that the general obligation might compel their liquidity against them. By taking measures to pay off their general debt load, they may see enhancements surprisingly profiled.

CREDIT REPAIR SERVICES

Various organizations professing to do credit fix have jumped up after some time. Keeping in mind that some may give benefits that can help shoppers, their endeavors' real aftereffects may be addressed. Now and again, credit fix may require the law, just like money related aptitude. Contingent upon the degree of the issue, it might require just tidying up mistaken assumptions, while in different cases, proficient intercession is required.

The expenses a credit repair organization charges can change. Commonly, there are two kinds of charges: an underlying arrangement expense and a monthly administration charge. The underlying expense can extend from $10 to $100, while the month to month expense normally runs in the range of $30 and $100 every month, albeit a few organizations charge more.

IS CREDIT REPAIR BAD?

Absolutely.

What's more, the law above promises it as well. The basic truth is that while there are numerous corrupt individuals on both sides of the credit fence (loan specialists, sellers, and repair organizations), the central right to challenge contests and remove things from your report is legitimate. For what reason does the credit repair business possess such a terrible name?

Reality? Since there is a lot of cash on all sides and because credit is such a significant product from numerous points of view, artful individuals of various kinds and stripes have found ways to exploit the credit system. This incorporates ruthless lenders and credit fix "facilities" that frequently guarantee to "fix" your credit medium-term while utilizing flawed techniques.

IS CREDIT REBUILDING EVEN CONCEIVABLE?

Truly, undoubtedly. I have utilized an assortment of exceptionally basic, extremely clear, and effective credit fix methodologies let alone reports, on more than one event. What's more, I gave myself "A" credit in under 4 months when it began as a "D", sometimes even an "F" over and over. The credit laws are set up, in all honesty, to favor you and me, and now is the best time to figure out how to fix your credit when there's no other option!

APPROACHES TO OBTAINING YOUR CREDIT REPORT

A credit report massively affects your life. If you are trying to get kudos for another vehicle, advance for another kitchen, or look for a mortgage, you can wager that the potential loan specialists have looked at your credit report.

Previously, getting a credit report was an entirely overwhelming errand. It was a very tedious procedure. Be that as it may, today with the web's assistance, you will have the option to acquire your virtual credit report in minutes. Another extraordinary advantage of acquiring these reports online is that you will get the report without paying any expenses. You will have the option to demand your credit report structure from every organization once a year. In case you want to make a significant purchase, for example, a house or a vehicle, it is easy to check the report at any rate once in a quarter of a year. This will assist you with the knowledge about the negatives that can occur in the report. Most of the time, most individuals do not give a lot of significance to this, resulting in various problems.

When you are checking your report quarterly, you will have the option to deal with the negatives that can happen, but if you are not doing it frequently, you may think it's difficult to expel the negatives. When you are confirming your report, it is essential to deal with even the least complex viewpoints. For example, you will have the option to locate some little obscure passages in the report, which can be a service charge, apportion bill, and so on. In such cases, it is critical to make these obscure passages known.

Now and again, you may observe some stuff on the report which don't belong there. This, you will come to know if you are playing out an intensive check to determine your report's status. Along these lines, if you find anything that you have cleared, make sure you make it obvious. Considering these little angles can assist you in making some great changes in your report.

If your credit report smells, you can hope to be denied or, in any case, pay a higher pace of intrigue. To this degree, guaranteeing your credit report is without mistakes is an easy decision. If you realize how to get a credit report, you can cross-check it for potential errors and screen your very own money-related conduct to improve it.

WHAT IS REMEMBERED FOR A CREDIT REPORT?

Regularly you can anticipate some close-to-home data, for example, past addresses, open records, date of birth, and your standardized savings number.

It also tells how much you take care of your tabs, the credit you may have remaining, what sort of obligations you may have, and how productive you are reimbursing on a month to month premise.

WHAT DOES THE CREDIT REPORT INFORM THE BANK ABOUT ME?

The credit report makes no official judgment—it is essentially an assortment of data recorded about your budgetary undertakings. The loan specialists themselves will draw decisions from the report, choosing whether you merit a punt or not.

If all my data is out there, for what reason do I need a credit report?

There are two main reasons why you should understand how to acquire a credit report. Right off the bat, there is consistently the likelihood that blunders have been made on the report, and such mistakes could be straightforwardly influencing the choice that banks make. You will have the chance to fix the blunders or clarify any mix-ups that have been made.

Furthermore, an acknowledged report goes about as a great reflection on how you handle your funds. Numerous individuals have thought of it as a manual for what they could improve later on. Thus, your credit report may be astounding a couple of years down the line if it isn't now.

HOW WOULD I ACQUIRE A CREDIT REPORT?

There are two prominent techniques. The first is to get in touch with one of your nation's credit offices and, for a little charge, they will send you a full report in the post.

Then again, there is a less difficult and quicker arrangement. You are now able to get your credit report in a flash on the web. You will have to pay a little charge, but certain administrations may furnish you with a free preliminary if you shop around.

CREDIT REPAIR WITHOUT DISPUTING

Now that you have dealt with any possible errors that might have plagued your credit, you are ready to move on to the tough stuff. This is the stage where you need to review your financial habits and figure out which ones are healthy and which ones are only hurting your credit score. It's not an easy process. Many of the mistakes we make are completely unintentional, but no less harmful to our financial security. Additionally, it can be tough to change the patterns that have long since become ingrained in our daily, weekly, and monthly routines. However, making these changes is necessary if you want to turn your credit around, as you have already seen how it gets with a negatively impacted score. At this point, your only options are to continue allowing your creditworthiness to deteriorate, further putting you into debts as you fail to qualify for credit lines and you get poor interest rates for those you do obtain, or you can make the tough changes that will set you on the path to future financial success.

Repairing your credit starts with making changes to the way you view and interact with your finances. If you continue to put things off, leave debts to pile up, and generally treat your credit like a secondary issue, it will continue to grow worse.

You want to shoot for long-lasting changes in the way you spend your money and the mentality you have when utilizing debt. If you are always looking to be conscientious about your score and your overall financial health, you will find it much easier to stick to making good credit decisions. However, the intention is only half the battle; the other half is learning what to do and getting it done.

If you try to repair your credit though you don't know how to go about doing it, you may waste time and money by failing to put your effort where it is most needed.

As a rule of thumb, target the big stuff first, and then move on to the things that are only having a minimal impact on your credit.

You want to avoid making common credit mistakes that will stagnate your process. Learn what to do and what not to do, and you will be halfway to putting this knowledge into practice and enjoying the benefits of an outstanding credit score.

Lifestyle Changes and Financial Strategies

Bringing your credit score up to a healthy number requires you to make some lifestyle changes. You may not be able to make frivolous purchases because you cannot afford to worsen your debt, or because you need to increase the cash you have at hand to pay your debts off with. You may also need to adjust the method by which you allocate funds for making payments and the way you utilize available lines of credit. Once you have made the appropriate changes and developed certain financial strategies that will make your relationship with money a much more positive one, you will find it easier to stay on top of credit payments. The following section contains a list of strategies you can use and actions you can take to increase your credit score directly and finally get you out of debt.

Pay Bills on Time

Late payments do your credit score no favors. You must get into the habit of paying your bills on time. Unpaid debts are hard to recover from, and routinely making late payments can make it hard to be on time for future payments. You want to correct these negative habits as soon as possible. If you have the money, but you struggle to get payments in on time, try marking them on your calendar or setting up automatic payments. Try to make payments for a given account at the same time each month. For example, you might make sure you always pay your rent on the 25th of the month, or you might pay your phone bill on the second Tuesday of every month. Once you get into the habit of making a few payments on time, you will be more inclined to remember them at the end of every billing period.

Pay More Than the Minimum

If you have the money available, you should try to pay more than your accounts' minimum payment. Having a balance remaining at the end of a payment period lets interest accrue on your debt, which can double or triple the amount you are paying depending on the APR and the cost of the debt. Interest can build up over time into some very steep costs – all the more reason you should avoid only paying the minimum. If you can pay even $10 or $15 more on an account, you can reduce the amount of interest you are charged and keep future payments lower.

Maintain Low Credit Card Balances

Using a large portion of your available credit hurts your credit score. It suggests a dependency on credit and an inability to pay off debts promptly. To counteract this, you should keep the balances on each of your credit cards low compared to your credit limits. You do not necessarily have to pay them off in full but aim to use under 30% of your available credit at any given time for the best credit score results. Many maxed out and nearly maxed out cards on your credit report can seriously hurt your score and make it hard to get approved for future cards.

Pay Maxed-Out Cards First

Like the point above, you should always prioritize any maxed out cards when deciding what to pay off first. You do not want to have any of your cards hit their credit limit if it is avoidable. Having a maxed-out card impacts your credit score much more severely than even a card that has 90% of its credit limit in use. Always try to pay down these cards before dealing with others, as they can hurt your score when left to linger.

CHAPTER 2:

Some Steps to Take To Repair Bad Credit

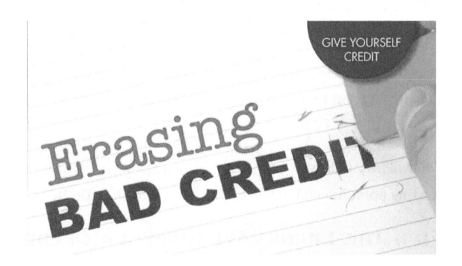

B eing able to fix your bad credit always seems like a wonderful dream because it seems impossible! You can at times discover that you want to improve your credit, but you simply do not know where you should start. It can be all too easy to say you want to change your credit but fail to do anything about it. So, where should you start? Is it even possible to fix your bad credit?

Well, to be honest, yes! It is possible to fix your bad credit but starting it can often get you stumped.

However, you must not panic because the following is a step-by-step guide to help you get started in changing your credit.

This is NOT a short fix; it takes time to fix your credit.

Usually, it takes at least six months before you see any kind of change, and around a year to see change for the better.

CHECK OUT YOUR CREDIT REPORT ONLINE

First, you do need to check your credit report carefully. You need to go over every little thing that is contained in your report. You do not want to miss a thing so check carefully and go over it a few times.

You will hear this over, and over, and over again, but it is a good starting point in helping you to fix your credit. Just Do It!

FIND THE ERRORS WITHIN YOUR CREDIT REPORT

Next, you need to find all those errors within your credit report and fix them. If you make a mistake in failing to make one payment, that is your fault.

However, it's a different story when it's someone else's mistake. If you find mistakes, you need to take note of each error and put it into dispute.

DISPUTE ANY ERRORS THAT YOU MAY FIND

To be honest, if you dispute what you think are errors, it could go a long way in helping you fix some parts of your credit.

Not all disputes will be considered, but if you find some incorrect errors there, you should get them fixed so that you have accurate information on your credit report.

CATCH UP ON ANY MISSED PAYMENTS

If you find that there are debts that you are lacking payment on or have missed a payment on several occasions, you need to catch up with them now!

You need to catch up with any payments you may have missed to improve your payment history greatly.

TRY TO GET REDUCED PAYMENTS

To be honest, some payments can be quite expensive. However, if you contact your creditors or lenders and ask them to lower the payments each month, it could help you repay the debt.

Remember, lenders want their money even if it means waiting a few more months to get the full amount back.

CALL A CREDIT AGENCY SO YOU DON'T HAVE TO STRUGGLE WITH REPAYMENTS

If you are in a very bad position with your finances and do not have the money to repay all your debts, you can consult a credit agency. Many agencies out there today can help you consolidate all your debts into one monthly repayment price. This cannot only help you to get rid of your debt but can also make your payments lower and more affordable.

MAKE SURE THAT YOU PAY EACH BILL AND EVERY DEBT ON TIME EVERY MONTH

A vital part of ensuring your credit improves is to make each month's payments on time. Do not miss out on any utility bills and remember your rent as well as every other cost.

If you keep making each payment, you will find that you can build a good period of repayment history. This all goes into improving your credit score. To help ensure you do not miss any payments, set up a standing order. This is when the payments are automatically taken from your bank and paid to each company when payment is due.

If you are choosing to pay the companies automatically, check your statements each month. You do not want to overpay especially if you have other bills to worry about. You need to ensure the right amount is taken out each time every month.

YOU CAN GET A LATE PAYMENT REMOVED FROM YOUR CREDIT HISTORY

If you have made a few late payments in the past, you may be able to get those removed from your credit report. Depending on how good your relationship with a company may be and how good your custom is, they may be willing to remove a late payment notice from your credit.

If you want to try this, why not contact the company in writing and ask if it would be possible. Removing even one late payment can be a great way to help improve your credit altogether. What is more, if you get one late payment removed from every company you have dealt with, it will all count towards a better credit score.

TRY TO GET A SECURED CREDIT CARD

Whenever a credit card is mentioned, you may panic a little because you instantly think it means taking it on. However, a secured credit card works a little differently from a normal credit card.

For a start, you have to put money into your account to use a secured credit card, which means you do not spend any more than you can afford and you do not have a bill at the end of the month!

This can be a great way to start building your credit. Remember, credit allows you to build your credit, which is true though it sounds strange.

That is why you need to try to establish a good form of credit. A secured credit card can be a great option if you can use it correctly.

UPGRADE TO AN UNSECURED CREDIT CARD

After you have made a few good constant months of payments with a secured card, you could try an unsecured card. This can be a way to up your credit. You do not necessarily need to choose a credit card, but rather a store card.

Having a departmental store card – just one – can be a fantastic way to up your credit. However, you still need to make every payment each month to have a good period of payment history.

TRY OUT A REAL CREDIT CARD

You could go for a normal credit card to help boost your credit. Though, do not try to use several credit cards at once. Stick to one and build small amounts on this so that you can repay each month. Even if it is only fifty dollars' worth of things each month, make sure you make each payment because it can go a long way to helping your credit. Also, make sure to pay off the minimum payment at least. However, do not get caught in this cycle; pay off as soon as possible when you can!

DO NOT CLOSE A CREDIT CARD

If you have old credit cards but haven't used them in a very long time, try to avoid having them closed.

Even though you might not want to use all three of your cards, you do not need to overspend on these.

You can easily put small charges on each to keep the accounts open. At the end of the month, pay the balance off and do the same for the next month.

Of course, you do not need to spend for the sake of keeping the account open. You can put a few purchases on the cards – it could be gas for your car, a meal at a restaurant, or just a sweater at a local store. Small is the key here – what you can afford!

DO NOT CO-SIGN FOR OTHERS WHILE YOU ARE TRYING TO FIX YOUR CREDIT SCORE

While co-signing for a new car for your boyfriend or friend may seem nice, it may damage your credit.

You cannot afford to have a co-sign loan on your credit because it makes you responsible for it. If that loan is not paid, you are responsible – which means you are the one who gets the bad credit!

Keep New Loan Applications Short and Straight to The Point

Searching for a loan for months is never a good thing. If you need to choose a loan, try to find one within a week or two. Do not have several applications running at one time because it can damage your credit. Instead, choose one and stick with the one you know you can be qualified for.

Keep Building Up Your Credit

Fixing bad credits can be simple, but only if you can establish new and good credit. Yes, you do need to take care of bad credits, but you also need to ensure that you establish new credits.

CHAPTER 3:

Secrets of Credit Repair

LOOK TO THE AVAILABLE CREDIT

A lot of people have when working on their credit is whether opening up a new line of credit or a new credit card would help them out. However, if you already have some credit going and you feel wrung dry, this is not the best action course. The reason is that you never want to end up using all of the available credit. This is a big mistake that will send up a lot of red flags to credit agencies all over. It is better to realize when too much is too much, and just work with what you have for now.

SECURED CREDIT

Secured credit is something that a lot of people are trying out now. It is a new method meant to help consumers who want to boost their scores, who do not have any credit to start with, or deal with poor credit. If you would like to seek out a boost in your score, and you think that you can handle the credit, then take a look at a secured credit card. These will be the same as a debit card, but with the function of a credit card. You will need to make payments every month, just like a credit card. With this, the credit agency will be able to see that you are in the process of building or repairing your credit.

DISPUTE

One of the smartest things that you can do to make your credit score go up is to dispute things that are not accurate on the credit report. Sometimes, the report that is out there for you will reflect some falsities that are going to harm your credit score. While it is difficult and may take some time, it is worth it to help you get that score up.

THE MISTAKES

If you are in the process of realizing that you need to repair your credit quite a bit, you must also realize that you should no longer make mistakes with your credit. Once you have dug that big hole, it is best to stop shoveling and learn how to stay as close to the surface as possible. This means do not try to take out any credit lines, make payments on time, and always check your report to make sure it is up to date and shows your efforts.

PAY DOWN YOUR DEBT

We will take a closer look at this one as we go through the process a bit more. The more you can pay down your debt, the better. This is not an easy process, and you will have to give things up and rein in your spending. You can pick out the budgeting or debt payment method that you want to work with, but as you make more of those payments along the way, you get things done on time, and as you are careful about getting the debt paid down, your score is going to go up. The rewards will be worth it in the end.

USE CREDIT SPARINGLY

Having a large balance on any of your cards (or even on all of them) will harm your credit score. It doesn't matter if you pay your bills in full each month or not. That large balance is going to harm the score.

The portion of the credit extended to you that you utilize will be sent out to the different credit bureaus, and it can make a big difference in your score. The more you can get the debt paid down, the better.

PAY THINGS OFTEN

To help you get the best credit score possible, you need to work with as little of the credit available to you as possible. If you can keep your credit utilization below 30%, although 10% is best, you will raise your score. Though if you have a low credit allowance, like $500, it will be even harder to manage this. One way to make sure that you can use the card and not harm your utilization rate is to make more than one payment in a billing cycle. You don't have to pay after each transaction if you don't want to, but you can make sure your utilization stays at the right spot if you are doing it regularly.

STRATEGICALLY OPEN ACCOUNTS

While you should not go crazy and open up a bunch of accounts all at once when you want to improve your credit score, you need to develop a strategic manner to handle these accounts to keep things safe and organized. Applying for any kind of credit is going to be something you do sparingly. These applications result in a hard inquiry on your report, and if they are recent, they will take a few points off.

If you are working with your low credit limits and your spending reduction isn't necessary, you could open up a new account or two to help you have more credit. Just remember that you should not increase your spending beyond what you can afford.

GET YOUR CREDIT REPORT

This first step is critical because your credit report will include all the credit information conveyed by your banks and other credit institutions you owe money from. Your credit report holds the secret of how you can proceed with your credit repair process. Many people do not think about getting a copy of their credit report unless they are faced with the hurdle of credit repair. But you need to understand that even when you have a credit standing, you will still need to regularly review your credit report to make sure that they do not contain any errors that can detrimentally affect your credit score.

GET IN TOUCH WITH ALL OF YOUR CREDITORS

After you have carefully reviewed your credit report and found no errors or inaccuracies, your next step in repairing your credit score is to contact the different credit institutions you have delinquent debts with. Your success in repairing your credit standing can depend on how quickly you can work with your creditors in solving your problems.

In most instances, creditors usually treat the recovery of their money from their debtors as their priority. Many people have been astonished upon learning that the creditors do accommodate requests for loan restructuring which can allow their debtors to have payment terms that are more reasonable for them. In certain cases, creditors can choose to reduce or even eliminate the unpaid balance interests. In other cases, creditors can even agree to lessen the principal balance itself if the debtors agree to pay the full balance amount immediately.

Always keep in mind that the primary objective of this exercise is to repair your credit standing. Ensure that you do not commit to any payment scheme with your creditors, which you think you are not capable of meeting. If you do so, you will only end up with much bigger problems than you started with. Suppose you keep missing your monthly payments even after your creditor has given you the chance to develop a better payment plan. In that case, your creditor may lose their trust in you and may no longer go for another restructuring of your loans.

You must agree to a new payment scheme that is truly workable for you. When you do this, your credit standing will be repaired more quickly.

Avoid Your Debt from Reaching Collection Agencies

When your creditors have finally determined that it is quite impossible to collect from you, they will be forced to sell your unpaid debt balances to collection agencies. This means that your creditors have decided that the possibility of collecting from you is so minimal that they are prepared to lose a portion of those unpaid loan amounts just to be able to collect something from you. The majority of debts sold to collection agencies are discounted for up to 50%, which means that your creditors will only be able to collect only half of what you owe them even if you make the full payment.

This is the worst possible thing that could happen to your credit and you will want to avoid it at all costs. When your creditors sell your unpaid loans to collection agencies, they have technically "written off" your loans in their books. When they do so, you will see that your credit report will receive the lowest possible rating. If you reach this lowest point in the credit cycle, it is advisable to take immediate actions to start your credit repair. When the collection agencies start calling you, they will force you to start paying your loans.

APPLY FOR A SECURED CREDIT CARD OF YOUR CHOICE

Secured credit cards are different from regular credit cards so that you will have to provide an initial deposit that has an equal amount as the credit limit. Simply stated, if you want a credit limit of $ 1,000, you will have to make an initial deposit of $200 to as much as $1,000 before your application can be approved. You will then give the credit card company the right to credit your bank account if you miss any of your monthly payments.

GET HELP FROM COMPANIES THAT SPECIALIZE IN CREDIT REPAIR

If you are in far deeper trouble and the above steps do not seem to help your situation, you can think about seeking help from a company with a specialization in credit repair. Of course, as expected, these companies will offer their services to "clean up your credit standing" in exchange for a fee.

CHAPTER 4:

Effective Strategies to Repair Your Credit

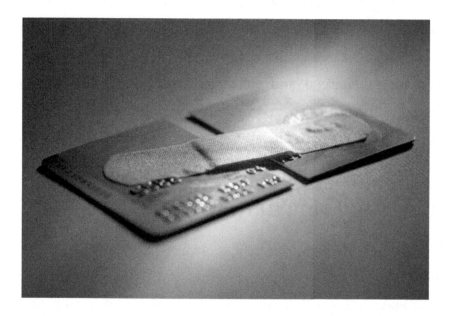

Fixing your credit is possible, and not as difficult as you have been made to believe. No matter how bad your credit score seems, the ways to magically boost it are, in fact, simple and practical. Contrary to common myths that a credit score may become so poor that it cannot be fixed, no credit score can be fixed. Whenever you find the need to fix one, apply the following strategies:

HIRE AN EXPERT

You can manage your company because you are quite intelligent, and in some way, everyone is. However, no matter how good you are, it is always nice to have an expert's opinions, especially in technical cases like this. You have learned hard lessons when your credit score drastically fell and you struggled to get it up, so it isn't such a bad idea to hear a couple of incisive words from a colossus. They would help with your budget, plans, financial decisions, and so forth. Services like these are sometimes charged and sometimes free, depending on the organization's motive or individual you approach. You may hire a credit or financial counselor, an economist, or a bankruptcy attorney, among other specialists.

WORK ON YOUR HISTORY

Since you are starting over, it is always a good idea to review your history. You should find out what you did wrong in each case and what was right and should have been enforced in your transactions. You should also learn about terms convenient for your business, policies you can subscribe to, and those you shouldn't ever consider no matter how juicy they seem. You should be on the lookout for errors you didn't note, who charged exorbitantly, whom you can bank on for further business deals, and so on.

BE UPDATED ON YOUR CREDIT SCORE

It is a new season, and you want to enjoy all the blessings it brings. One way you can do this is to start monitoring your credit report, so it doesn't ever go bad again. No matter how bad it seems already, you are bound to get the best out of it when you are updated with your credit scores and your credit report in general.

You must think about your credit position and make informed decisions in your finances every single time. Gradually, you can boost your credit scores this way. Besides, you need to keep your eyes on the credit report and your credit bureaus.

You deserve a spick-and-span record this time, and you shouldn't avoid lapses that can ruin that. So, be updated on your credit information and consider that each time you make financial decisions.

DO NOT CLOSE YOUR OLD ACCOUNTS

Whether your accounts have become delinquent or have gotten to a point wherein you don't want to associate with them anymore, it is always recommended that you still keep them open in some way.

Keeping accounts open can serve as an advantage in further credit transactions to prove your experience with loans.

However, if you must close an account, be sure there is no debt or balance to be covered in it as that can be a big minus to your new account. It is highly recommended that you avoid creating new credit records at this point.

REACH OUT TO YOUR CREDITORS

Now, this is interesting. Many people do not see the need to reach out to their creditors after their loans have been activated. Especially if they can afford the charges and there seems no reason to be in touch. However, that's not right. There can be cases wherein you can't pay your monthly dues. Sometimes, you may have huge plans or investments that can't wait till the coming month, and your best way to hit this is your monthly debt. If you are in touch with them, establish that you appreciate their business interaction and do not mind relating them beyond the current contract. You will be glad you did because you can count on them to be lenient at such moments and find some way to ensure your credit score is not affected. Many business transactions are conducted on the grounds of a good relationship between the key figures in the business.

BE PATIENT

Your credit score didn't deteriorate in hours; you should expect to rebuild it to take some time. The different steps you take will not yield many positive results immediately, certainly not as much as you'd like, but it's no reason to despair.

It is certainly possible to build it again and it will happen if you are consistent. Do not mind how long the process seems – it always works for consistent, as Harry Hans of Financial times would say.

AVOID UNNECESSARY CREDITS

You surely remember that the federal court on Bankruptcy declared in 2013 that over 70% of unsecured debts are incurred on purchases that could be avoided. You don't want to add a penny to that percentage. It is why you should avoid purchasing items that do not appear in your budget. You should also limit the rate at which you explore markets and rake home some niceties, courtesy of your credit card. You can hit a nice score again if you take those tips. None of these are new principles. They are all simple and practical, so ensure you always remember them.

PAY-TO-DELETE STRATEGY

If you have derogatory items in your credit report, you can opt to pay the unpaid credit balance only if the creditor agrees to delete the items from your credit report. As I already mentioned, don't agree with a $0 balance appearing on your credit report since this taints your reputation. As a rule of thumb, less is more in this section; the fewer items you have here, the better off for you. This method works through the idea that your report doesn't show whether you have had any history of bad credit in the derogatory items section. This will ultimately improve your rating. The idea is to ensure that whatever amount you agree to pay doesn't show up as your last activity date. If the creditor only cares about their money, why should they bother telling the world you have finally paid?

In most instances, the creditors often write off debts within just 2 years of constantly defaulting. This information is sold in bulk to a collection company for some pennies or a dollar. This means that the collection companies will be just fine if you even pay a fraction of what you ought to pay. Whatever you pay, they will still make money! This makes them open to negotiations such as pay-to-delete since they have nothing to lose anyway.

Therefore, only use the pay-to-delete approach at this level and not any other. The only other way around it for the collection company is a judgment, which can be costly, so you have some advantage.

Additionally, you can use this strategy when new negative items start showing up in your report that could hurt your reputation as a credit consumer.

Also, since the creditors will often sell the same information to multiple collection companies, you might probably start noting the same debt reported by several companies; use pay-to-delete to get them off your report.

You can also use this strategy if you have not successfully got items off your credit report using other methods. Opting to go the dispute way might only make the process cyclic, cumbersome, tiresome, and frustrating; you don't want to get into this cycle.

Now that you know when to use this method, understanding how the entire process works is critical. To start with, ensure that you get an acceptance in writing if they agree to your terms; don't pay without the letter! After you agree, allow about 45 days for the next credit report to be availed to you by your credit monitoring service. These companies have the legal power to initiate the deletion process, so don't accept anything less such as updating the balance; it is either a deletion or nothing. If they try to stall the process by saying that they cannot delete, mention that it will only take about 5 minutes to fill the Universal Data Form. Don't worry if one company doesn't seem to agree with your terms, another one will probably show up and gladly take the offer.

In any case, what do they have to gain when they keep your debt when you are willing to pay? Remember that the records will only be kept for 7 years, so these companies have no other choice if 2 years have already passed. However, don't use this as an excuse for not paying your debts since the creditors can sue you to compel you to pay outstanding amounts.

This process aims to ensure that whatever bad experience you have with one creditor doesn't make the others make unfavorable decisions on your part.

Note: don't be overly aggressive with creditors who have a lot to lose in the process, especially recent creditors since they can probably sue you. Your goal is only to be aggressive with creditors barred by the statute of limitations from suing you in court. You don't want to find yourself in legal trouble to add to your existing problems. Try and remain as smart as possible and make all the right moves to help you repair your credit at the earliest.

Pay-to-delete isn't the only option available to you; you can use other strategies to repair your credit.

CHECK FOR FDCPA (FAIR DEBT COLLECTION PRACTICES ACT) VIOLATIONS

The law is very clear on what collection agencies can do and what they cannot do as far as debt collection is concerned. For instance:

1. They should not call you more than once in a day unless they can prove that their automated systems accidentally dialed it.
2. They cannot call you before 8:00 a.m. or after 9:00 p.m.

3. They cannot threaten, belittle, or yell at you to make you pay any outstanding debts.

4. They cannot tell anyone else other than your spouse why they are contacting you.

5. The best way to go about this is to let them know that you record all their calls.

6. They cannot take more money from your account than you have authorized if they do an ACH.

7. They are also not allowed to send you collection letters if you have already sent them a cease and desist order.

If you can prove that collection companies violate the laws, you should file a complaint with the company then have your lawyer send proof indicating the violations; you can then request that any outstanding debt be forgiven. You need to understand that the law is on your side in such circumstances. If the violations are major, the collection companies could be forced to pay fines of up to $10,000 for these violations.

So, if your debt is significantly lower than this, you could be on your way to having your debt cleared since these companies would rather pay your debt than pay the fine. Every violation of the Fair Debt Collection Practices Act is punishable by a fine of up to $1000, which is payable to you, so don't just think of this as something that cannot amount to anything repairing your credit is concerned.

LOOK FOR ERRORS ON YOUR CREDIT REPORTS

Your credit report should be free of errors. Even the slightest thing as reporting the wrong date of last activity on your credit report is enough to damage your credit. Your last date of activity has a profound effect on your credit rating. If the write-off date is different from what has been reported, you can dispute the entry to have it corrected to reflect your credit's actual status. However, keep in mind that the credit bureaus will, in most instances, confirm that the negative entry is correct even if this is not the case, which means that they will not remove the erroneous item.

You must put in efforts to get them on the right track. To get them to comply, you must inform them that the law requires them to have a preponderance of their systems to ensure that these errors do not arise. Therefore, the mere fact of confirming the initial error is not enough. Inform them about the notice (summons) and complaint to understand that you are serious about the matter. Once they have an idea of your stance, they will put in efforts to do the right thing. The bureaus don't want any case to go to court since this could ultimately prove that their systems are weak or flawed, which means that they will probably be in big trouble. So, try and drive a strong point across so that they understand you mean business. The mere exchange of emails will not do, and you must send them details on how strong your case will be. This will make them understand their position and decide to help you avoid going to court. This will, in turn, work to your advantage in making them dig deeper into the issue. However, this method will only work if you are certain that an error was made. You will also require proof for it and cannot simply state that there was an error.

REQUEST PROOF OF THE ORIGINAL DEBT

Suppose you are certain that the credit card has been written off for late payment. In that case, the carriers (Capital One and Citibank) likely cannot find the original billing statements within 30 days, which they are required by the law to respond. This, in effect, allows you to have whatever entry you have disputed removed from the credit report as if it never happened.

Another handy approach is to request for the original contract that you signed to be provided. This is to prove that you opened that particular credit card in the first instance. As you do this, don't just ask for "verification" since this just prompts the collection agency to "verify" that they received a request for collection on an account that has your name on it. Therefore, as a rule of thumb, ensure that you state clearly that you want them to provide proof of the debt, including providing billing statements for the last several months and the original contract that you signed when opening the credit card account.

PAY THE ORIGINAL CREDITOR

When your debt is sold to collection agencies, you will probably risk having new items showing up on your credit report, which can further hurt your credit rating. However, you can stop by sending a check with the full payment of any outstanding amount to the original creditor.

You just send proof of payment to that collection agency and any other, then request them to delete any derogatory items they have reported from your credit report.

It is always a good idea to be in direct contact with your creditor or creditors. Many of these agencies will be fully equipped to cheat you and follow through on plans to have your report show bad credit scores.

It is up to you to try and remove these "middlemen" and do the payment yourself. You could also agree to pay a portion of the money to the creditor as full payment for the sum (the pay-to-delete strategy).

Under the federal law, if the original creditor accepts any payment as full payment for any outstanding debt, the collection agency must remove whatever they have reported. This will only work if the original creditor accepts the payment; it is possible for some of the checks you pay to the original creditor to be returned to you.

IDENTIFY THEFT CLAIM

Over 16 million Americans are victims of identity theft. This is a large population so anyone could be a victim. Identity theft is a crime, which involves the police so ensure you are ready to go this route. If you are sure that your score has been ruined because of identity theft, you can use this method. Abusing this method could land you into trouble with the law. Here is how to dispute using the method:

Step 1: Report the matter to the police then get a copy of your report from the local sheriff (you will need this report later)

Step 2: File the dispute with FTC

Step 3: Go on to dispute with various credit bureaus.

Step 4: Set up an identity theft alert (be sure to know what this means in terms of your access to credit)

LOOK OUT FOR ERRORS IN THE REPORT

I mentioned that 93% of the credit reports have been proven to have errors. Look out for any of these then file a dispute. Such things like the last date of activity, write-off date, wrong account name or number, and others could be enough to taint your credit. Don't overlook any of that. If the report has an error, don't be discouraged by the credit bureau's stalling tactics; mention the Notice (Summons) and complaint to make them know that you know what the law requires of them. The bureaus wouldn't want to have their systems investigated and proven to be weak/flawed so this strategy can compel them to correct errors thus boosting your credit.

SETTLE YOUR DEBT

Total debt owed accounts for up to 30% of the credit score so don't overlook this. This includes personal loans, car loans, and credit utilization. You should also calculate the credit utilization ratio (the balance you carry in your revolving fund compared to your credit).

As your credit utilization increases, your credit score goes down; aim to keep your credit card balances no more than 30% of your credit card limit. You should even aim for zero balances since this means a higher credit score. Combine this strategy with the pay-to-delete strategy.

To pay your debts, you can use the snowballing or avalanching strategies. Snowballing involves paying off debts with the lowest balance first then closing them as you move up to the bigger debts.

Avalanching involves paying debts starting from those with the highest interest rates as you move down.

SETTLE YOUR BILLS PROMPTLY

Payment history accounts for 35% of your credit score, making it one of the score's biggest determinants. This is pretty straight forward; when you pay your bills on time, your score will improve. You could even set up automatic payments to ensure that you won't miss payments since the amounts are deducted from your account. The biggest contributors to this include collections, bankruptcies, and different late payments. You should note that the recent delinquencies have a greater effect than the old ones; 70% of the score is determined by whatever has happened within the past 2 years.

MIX/SPREAD YOUR CREDIT

This usually affects your credit score by up to 10%. Having more types of credit signifies that you can handle your finances properly making you creditworthy especially if you have a good payment history.

CHAPTER 5:

How to Pay Off Debt

Many folks suffer a financial crisis at some point. They may have to deal with overspending, losing a job, a family member's illness, or personal illness. These financial problems can be and usually are, overwhelming. To make these situations worse, most people don't even know where to solve these financial dilemmas. Our goal here is to shine some light on the strategies to help you.

Accumulating basic consumer debt will chain you into slavery and you could spend your life held down by your obligations to repay these loans.

Who do you work for? I don't care what you say, the real answer is your creditors if you are currently stuck paying the debt.

We are all sold images and lifestyles hundreds of times per day to provoke this materialistic behavior – its many forms of "dumb debt" you can get trapped in.

What type of credit should you get? That depends on what you plan to do with the money. The most used types of credit are secured and signature credits.

For smaller loans, there's no need for that, as no institution would like to end up with a store of household items, so they lend you money or issue a credit card in your name simply based on the strength of your credit so far.

There is hope; you as the borrower have many options to get rid of debt. You can take advantage of budgeting and other techniques, such as debt consolidation, debt settlement, credit counseling, and bankruptcy procedures.

You just have to choose the best strategy that will work for you. When choosing from the various options, you must consider your debt level, discipline, and plans.

THE GOOD DEBT

Some people find it hard to live debt-free; they'll always have some debts to pay off. While some debts are discouraged, good debt is considered the money you borrow to pay for things that you need or things that increase in value. On the flip side, bad debt arises from things that you only want and often decreases in value.

Of course, debt isn't a bad thing; it's just how you use the money that matters.

For a good debt, you will always have a good reason to justify it, and a developed plan for paying it so that you can clear the debt as quickly as possible. An individual with good debt will also have the cheapest methods of borrowing money. They will do this by looking at the borrowing method, rate of interest, credit amount, and appropriate charges. Sometimes, it may imply a deal with the least possible interest rate, but sometimes, it may not.

EXAMPLES OF GOOD DEBT

Getting business loans

While this may not be seen as good debt, borrowing money to begin a business or expand a business is perhaps a great idea if the business is thriving. After all, you need money to make more money, right?

Sometimes, you may have to borrow capital to employ new people, purchase a new device, pay for advertisement, or even develop the first new widget you designed. If you borrow this money to expand the business or increase income, this will count as good debt.

WHAT IS BAD DEBT?

Bad debt is that which depletes your wealth and isn't affordable. Plus, it provides no means to pay for itself. Bad debts may have no realistic repayment plans and usually deplete when people buy things on impulse. If you aren't sure whether you can repay the money, then don't borrow the money because that will be a bad debt.

THE KEYS TO GETTING RID OF DEBT

Debt is a way of life for some Americans. We owe money for houses, cars, possessions (from furniture to clothes), and education. Many Americans are so intensely in debt that they don't know how much they owe anyone; worse yet, sometimes they don't even remember the cause of their debt.

First, attack your debts with significant expenses

This includes credit cards where you can pay high minimum payments and high-interest rates. First, pay off the credit card balance with the highest interest rates.

Continue to make your minimum payments for the cards with the lowest interest rates but focus on the highest interest rates. When expensive cards pay off, try withdrawing balances from other cards.

Second, contact your creditors

If you're late or have trouble making your minimum payments, contact your credit card company. While you can make all payments on time, you can get two benefits by contacting your card issuer. First, you can negotiate lower prices or more favorable terms. Second, they can recommend other options that can reduce the damage to your credit rating.

Third, consolidate your debt as much as possible

You can do this in several ways. One option is to change the balance from one credit card to another at a lower rate (consider the transfer fees before choosing that option). Another option, if you have your own home, is to get an apartment loan or a line of credit which, in addition to being lower than credit cards, must have a lower interest rate that offers deductions tax.

Essentially, you can also consider a secured loan that provides value in another form of property, such as your vehicle.

Fourth, don't sacrifice your retirement savings

Paying down debt should be a high financial priority, but cutting back on what you save for retirement may not be the smart thing to do, especially if it becomes a habit in the long run. You may be able to borrow from your pension fund at a lower interest rate, which will allow you to continue saving for your pension once the debt is cleared.

While lending money may be the American way, it can be a heavy burden. Follow these four steps to weigh the load or at least reduce it to a more manageable level.

USING CONSOLIDATION OR SETTLEMENT STRATEGIES TO PAY DOWN DEBTS

Debt consolidation is another strategy that can be used to manage your debts. It involves combining two or more debts at a lower interest rate than you are currently at.

It is worth doing your research and making some phone calls to see if a company is willing to work with you. If you can lower your monthly bill to a manageable level, at a reasonable interest rate, that can make all the difference in handling your debt.

Like many strategies, you have had the option of settling your debts with companies for decades.

Lenders always want as much money as you can give them versus being shafted for the entire amount in a bankruptcy. It is just that consolidation and settlement options rose in popularity during the recent financial crisis making it appear in more articles and news pieces than ever before.

If you have savings to pay off your debts, then start with the most expensive. Otherwise, utilize settlement options to reduce the amount owed if you pay a certain amount right now. As long as the account shows paid in full, your scores will increase with strong payment history. It doesn't matter if you needed to use debt settlement strategies to make the debt end. It just matters that you have paid the debt off instead of letting it go into arrears.

Negotiate with Credit Companies

Another thing a lot of people do not know is that you can negotiate with credit companies. You can take the collection letter they send you, or a past due notice that has been sent to you, and discuss it with them. In many cases, they will take a lower amount than what's on the bill just so that they can guarantee they'll get something

Let's say you owe Discover $1,000. They want to get their money, so they send you a past due notice. But for several months you've ignored that past due notice and now they've sent it to collections.

The collections agency may offer you a settlement. Maybe they say they'll take $900 if you just pay it to them right then and there. You have the opportunity to call them and request that they take a lesser amount.

If you talk to the collection agency and agree to take a lesser amount you will have to send that payment in full. Ensure that when you send them the check you write out the words 'paid in full' on the check. Make a copy of the check for your records as well. Once they cash that check your account is legally considered to be paid in full and they are no longer able to come after you for more money.

Cut the Credit Cards

If you're looking to save some money, you need to make sure you're spending less. That means getting rid of all those credit cards. If you're able to avoid the temptation to purchase things you can put one credit card in the back of your purse or wallet. Choose a card that will work anywhere such as a major credit card company. This is for emergencies only. An emergency doesn't mean you found something that you want to have. It means that you have run out of gas, or your car broke down and needs to be towed.

The rest of the credit cards you decide to keep should be locked up somewhere in your home. Put them in a safe or lockbox.

This way you have to actively think about getting the card out again before using it. This will keep you from using the card in a spur of the moment fashion and will ensure that you still have it available if necessary.

The best thing to do is make one to two small purchases on your credit card every few months. Try to space out using different cards so that none of them gets taken but you don't owe very much money each month. You want to keep the amount negligible, meaning it is low enough to affect your overall budget. This will let you keep the card but, at the same time, it won't completely break the bank.

Talking to Creditors

Tell them the reason why you're having a difficult time paying the debts. Most companies will negotiate a modified payment plan so monthly payments become more manageable. If you wait for the accounts to go into default, it can and most likely affect your credit score negatively, which is what we're looking to avoid, because once in default, the collector will start calling.

Taking Advantage of Debt Relief Services

A debt settlement company will put your deposits in a bank account managed by a third party. Although you own the funds and accrued interests, the account manager will charge a fee for services because they'll be the ones to transfer funds from your account to the creditors' accounts.

Before signing up for a debt relief service, you must know the exact price and terms that the company offers. You also need to know how long it will be before you can expect to get results. The debt relief service firm must also inform you how much the negotiated debt is and the amount of money you need to have in the designated bank account before the company can tender an offer to each creditors. Also, they must inform you about the probable consequences if you fail to make the payments.

There are cases when creditors report settled debts to the Internal Revenue Service. Unless you are insolvent, the IRS may consider savings from debt relief service as taxable; meaning they may consider the income generation's situation. As such, they should talk to an accountant. We don't want the IRS after us when we just got rid of the collection agency's calls!

It may sound like all the debt relief companies are out to scam us, but they're not.

We, the consumer, just need to be aware of all the steps involved to make an informed choice about whether this particular option is right for our situation.

Ideally, if you want a company with a positive Better Business Bureau rating, you must know how much each service will cost and how long you'll have to wait to get the expected results. You should read any contract you enter thoroughly and get every promise in writing.

Credit Counseling

Credit counseling is a service offered by some organizations to borrowers seeking advice on managing their finances. It usually includes budgeting, workshops, and educational resources. A counselor must receive training and certification in budgeting, money and debt management, and consumer credit. He or she must tackle your financial situation and offer help in creating a personalized plan. Usually, the first session can last for an hour or more.

HOW TO PAY DOWN DEBT

A simple look online will show us that there are so many ways that you can pay off your debt, and they are all going to work in slightly different manners. If they have you paying down your debt and ensuring that you don't take on new debt, they are good options to work with without a bunch of other risks in the process. You can choose the one that makes the most sense to you.

We are going to spend some time, not looking at a specific plan that you can use to pay down your debt, rather, we are going to focus more on the basic steps that you can take, no matter the kind of debt repayment plan you are using, to help make paying your debts off a little bit easier in the long run. Some of the steps that we can use here include:

Stop with the New Debt

You are never going to get out of debt if you just keep adding to your debt number. It is always best to stop with the new debt and find ways to limit it as much as possible. While most people are not getting the right kind of training on handling money, you may feel like it is impossible to get out of debt unless you are willing and able to go through the retraining process for your financial habits now.

You need to get right into the mix and stand against all the marketers interested in trying to take your hard-earned money or offering you some easy financing. Keep in mind that while marketers try to convince you otherwise, you don't need more stuff to make you happy. What you need instead is financial peace of mind.

So, instead of having the temptation around and taking on more debt, cut up your credit cards so you can't use them. Sit down and come up with a budget, and then stick with it. Turn off the social media and the advertisements so that they cannot control you any longer. This helps to limit the chances when you are tempted to purchase something that you do not need.

Rank the Debt Using Interest Rates

For this one, we will list out all the debts that we owe and list out the interest rate that comes with them. The highest interest rate needs to be put at the top of the list.

That will be the one that you work on paying off first. Paying off the high-interest debt will be the key to what is known as the stack method of debt payoffs and can get that debt gone quickly.

Other methods work well, but these often focus on motivational factors and can be slower at getting the work done. Interest will be a powerful weapon, and right now, the banks or other companies are using it against you if you don't pay things off. Interest will increase the amount that you have to pay back in the end, and often we are not fully aware of how much that ends up being.

We have a credit card with a $10,000 limit on it, and there is a 20% interest. You decide to pay the minimum amount of $200 a month. In the end, it is going to take about 9 years and 8 months if you don't put any more money into it. This means that you are going to end up paying the bank $11,680 extra in just interest.

See if You Can Lower Interest Rates

In some cases, it is possible to lower your credit interest rates with a balance transfer. You need to be careful with this one, but it means that you will move your debt to another bank, and they will offer you a lower interest rate to try and get your business.

If you are going to do this, you don't want just to jump right in. Make sure that you will pay the amount off rather than end up with two credit cards that are maxed out, and you should shop around to get the lowest amount of interest for the longest duration possible. Read through all the terms and conditions that show up and make sure the bank doesn't have hidden fees or other issues that you need to be worried about.

Create Your Budget

This is where we are going to work on improving our financial control. Bring out a pen and paper and write down what your total income is, after-tax, and then write down all the expenses that you have. This includes any extras that you have and the minimum payments that you owe as well. We can cut these out later, but we just want a full look at it to start.

We can then look at all the expenses there and rank them based on their importance. Look at the items near the bottom of that list and determine if they are worth cutting to keep you financially stable. The objective here is to create a plan where you can get the expenses lower than the income.

You also need to figure out how much you are willing to spend on all aspects of your life. You can set aside amounts for eating out, groceries, rent, buying clothes, and more. Once you allocate that money, realize that you are not allowed to dip into other areas. You may want to consider working with a fun account that will be there just for you to spend on something that doesn't usually fit into the budget. This allows you a bit of freedom without derailing the budget.

Even if your expenses are already below your income when you start, this doesn't mean that you can just stop there. You want to make sure that you can cut your budget down as much as possible. This allows you to make more money each month and throw it at your debt payments, making you more efficient at getting that credit score in line faster than ever.

Create Your Repayment Schedule

The first part that we need to focus on here is covering at least the minimum on all the debts you have. If you miss anything, even if you are trying to pay off another debt faster, you will incur a lot of feed and more, and these can add up quickly. Make at least this payment each month.

Then, you take the debt that has the highest interest rate, and you will use the extra that is found in your budget and pay that extra towards that biggest debt. As you see, the official minimum payment goes down, and you will be able to add the extra to your target debt. This will help you to pay down the debt fast, especially if you put any extra money towards that each month.

When that first debt is all done, it is time to move on to the second-highest interest rate debt. With this one, you will take the minimum payment you were doing before, along with the minimum payment available from the debt you paid off, and any extra you were paying. All that goes towards the second debt, which can be paid off in no time.

We continue this process, taking the extras that are used from one debt and throwing them at the next one on the line, with the payments getting bigger and paying things off faster as we go along. While the first debt may take some time to complete because you are also paying for all of the other debts, the last few will be paid off in no time by the time you get to them.

Be Kind to Yourself

Keep in mind that paying off debts, even though it is so good for your credit score, is not something that you will be able to do overnight. During this process, which can be a long one, you will feel that your resolve is being tested quite a bit. You may have an emergency that happens, like a car breaking down, and you will have to change your plans.

This is a normal part of life and not something to get frustrated about. The important thing to remember here is not to give up and revert to your old habits, or you will never get that debt paid off. Be kind to yourself when things in life happen, and don't give up. You will get those debts paid off in no time if you are willing to do the work.

We want to work so hard at paying down our debts and making sure that they don't stick around for a long time because it helps us with our credit scores while freeing up more money to do what we want. When our utilization rates are lower because we pay things off and don't miss payments because the amounts are not as high as they were, our credit score will go through the roof.

LIFESTYLE CHANGES TO ACHIEVE FINANCIAL FREEDOM

It's time to let go of the credit-damaging habits that put you in the financial situation that you are in at present. Financial freedom is not impossible to achieve no matter how dire your debt situation is now. You can start practicing lifestyle changes now even as you are attempting to repair your credit.

Keep it simple

With all the modern amenities today, it is easy to get lured into consumerism. People tend to buy things they do not need. Go back to the basics and limit your spending to only the necessities. Pack your lunch and snacks not to have to buy your food from a restaurant or the cafeteria. Make your coffee and put it in a thermos so you can have your caffeine throughout the day without having to go to the neighborhood coffee shop. Walk instead of taking a cab. Wear mix and match clothes instead of the latest designer threads. Simplifying your lifestyle will help you steer clear of debt, save money, and eventually be financially free.

Follow your budget

Any financially responsible individual should have a budget. Know how much income you are receiving and how much money you are spending. Set aside a percentage of your income for emergency expenses and long-term savings.

Remember that you are not supposed to spend on something you cannot afford. This is something that credit cards allow you to do. If you are to swipe that credit card, make sure you have enough on-hand to pay for that purchase. This brings us to the next practice.

Pay everything in full and on time

When you follow your budget, you are sure that you can pay for everything in full and on time. Everything should be accounted for when you do your budget so there should be no problem making your payments. You can use the envelope technique to put your money in envelopes marked with the budget items they are supposed to be allocated for. This way, you are sure that the money in a particular envelope goes to the expense it is budgeted for.

Pare down your credit

The many offers for credit cards with all sorts of freebies and perks could be tempting for many people. It is not advisable to have more than a couple of credit cards activated at any time.

You are likely to rack up a considerable amount of debt when you do this. Keep your credit cards to about 2 or 3, one of which can be an international card if you travel a lot. Keep your balances low. If you practice #3, you should not have any outstanding balance left every time you make your monthly repayment.

Watch your debt to credit ratio

Keep your debt-to-credit ratio lower than 10%. This refers to the amount that you owe versus your total credit limit. If your total credit limit is $10,000, you should not have an outstanding balance of over $1,000. Just because you are given a higher limit on your credit card does not mean that you have the license to max it out. It's a sure way to get caught in debt obligation. The practices above should help you reduce your debt-to-credit ratio to a minimum.

There is so much more for you to enjoy in life when you are debt-free and financially free. You do not have to worry about missing opportunities or not being eligible for things you know you deserve. You can live your life without unnecessary financial obligations. Free yourself now by repairing your credit, rebuilding your credit, and practicing wise financial management.

CHAPTER 6:

What is Section 609?

WHAT IS THE CREDIT DISPUTE **609** LETTER?

You may remove negative items from the credit report based on Section 609. A lot of people have been successful in the process, boosting their credit score. The process involves a written letter asking for the verification of every piece of information in your file hoping that something wasn't properly documented.

If the creditor failed to document something properly, no legal choice is there but to remove the negative items from the credit report.

HOW DOES A 609 LETTER WORK?

Now that you've reviewed your credit reports, credit scores, and credit history, you're ready to start thinking about what you can do to start pushing it upwards. Take each category of the FICO credit score, look at your history, and ask how you can improve that category.

You should begin by grouping problems you identified from your credit report review in a way that makes the most sense to you.

Consider creating a separate email account for your credit rating efforts. It will make it easier to keep related emails organized.

Here's one approach to organizing your tasks:

Quick and easy

If you have some credit inquiries that will expire soon, there's nothing you need to do except be careful about applying for new credit. Using some of your savings to reduce your debt load on a credit card that's near its limit is pretty simple, so long as you have the money to do so.

Moderate effort

If you found any discrepancies in any of your credit reports, you should contact the appropriate credit reporting company to see if you can get the error corrected. Remember, both the credit reporting companies and creditors are responsible for correcting inaccurate or incomplete information in your credit report, according to the FTC. Each of the three companies concerned has web pages specifically for customer disputes.

More effort

You can probably get a creditor to remove a late payment from your account record (more on this in a few lines). Another strategy you can consider is to take out a debt consolidation loan (more on this in a few lines too). It's a riskier strategy, so it needs to be carefully considered. If you've found a discrepancy in your credit report, writing a letter to the responsible credit reporting company should be one of the first things you do. The FTC even provides you with a sample letter at its web site. The FTC recommends you send the letter via certified mail "return receipt requested." It also says to include copies (not originals) of any relevant documents or receipts you have. It can also help send a copy of the page from your credit report with the item(s) circled.

While you can probably get things done via company websites, going the paper route gives you a physically documented record of your efforts. While you hopefully won't need it, hard evidence can be easier to work with and be more reliable than electronic records.

Get Your Stuff Together

It helps to be organized. Create a binder or file and start gathering any records that will help you make your case with the various companies you're going to need to communicate with. Make sure you have either web sites or email addresses for your creditors. Small businesses might not offer much when it comes to web sites, but you can count on the major credit card companies to have functional web sites that include ways to contact them for help or disputes. They usually have live support available online too. Remember, if you're communicating in real-time, be prepared ahead of time and have at least an outline of what you want to cover in your call. It is one advantage of using the mail to make your dispute, and you're much more likely to submit all the necessary proof. Make sure you have the originals of everything before you send in your dispute.

Your Checklist

Put together a checklist with deadlines to help keep you on track. Organize by the approach you like best. You can go from easy to hard, get going on the stuff that will take longer to respond on, and then knock off the faster stuff, so while the slow-moving chores are winding their way through the mail or a company bureaucracy, you can be getting things done.

Removing late payment codes: try to get as many of these removed as you can. Late payments take seven years to clear from your credit history, so trying to get as many as you can be removed can be a big help.

Correcting errors: If you are correcting misspellings, incorrect information, and erroneous accounts. Credit bureaus have 30 days to investigate your complaint. You can use the mail system or web site for Equifax or TransUnion. Experian only accepts requests online. You can find phone numbers, web addresses, and mail addresses for each company (if offered) here. One thing to look at extra strictly is anything listed by collections agencies. Consumer debt has a legal expiration date. Once that date has passed, you can't be forced to pay it. Collection agencies can still attempt to collect that debt, and they can even sell the debt to other collectors who will then try their luck collecting the debt. In the process, the dates recorded for that debt can be misreported, requiring correction. Of course, if a debt collector contacted you and you agreed to pay anything back (whether you paid any money or not), the clock on the debt begins from that point on.

Reducing debt ratios on credit cards: try to avoid having any tickets that are near their limits if you can. Considering transferring a balance if you can do so without doing anything to make your report worse (such as applying for a new card to shift the balance). Paying down the cards is ideal if you have the money.

Disputing items: this is a little different than correcting errors. Here, you're trying to get things off your report that may be justified. Still, if you can convince the creditor to remove the item, it's to your advantage, and let's face it, it's not like you're going to bully a big credit card company into doing something it doesn't want to do. Even disputing an old negative charge can sometimes pay off simply because the creditor may not respond.

Clearing civil judgments: these also appear on your credit history, so if you can pay them off or get them discharged, it will benefit your credit score.

DOES A 609 LETTER IMPROVE MY CREDIT?

While one's economic situation is different from another person's, most people may be in some debt at a particular time. For instance, you may have small debts such as in-store financing or credit card bills, while others may have large ones such as mortgages and loans. This translates that almost everyone is most likely dependent on having a specific amount of credit. Confidence can be useful for some things.

As mentioned earlier, your credit report, which is held by a credit bureau, is significant to your credit status.

The credit bureau will send you a notification when you are in default or missed payments to your creditors. Once you receive such notices, expect that you are in for a poor credit rating.

There are various steps involved in effective credit repair. These steps are particular to the situation of an individual. One of the most common actions that people in a bad credit situation take is debt consolidation.

If you are attempting to have your credit repaired, it is a principle to act as quickly as possible. Once you miss out on payments to your creditors, your credit rating will be damaged almost immediately. The more you continuously miss your payments, the more damaged your credit rating will be.

You might be one of the numerous people who get confused that credit is simply "good" or "bad," and once you are in trouble with a creditor, it is a futile effort to repair it. On the contrary, even if you are in a bad credit situation, credit repair enables you to pay off your debts in the quickest way possible. However, most people avoid any credit repair strategies because, first of all, they do not have money to pay their debts. For instance, you may have an unfortunate economic situation, which is why you missed out on your payments. This is the reason why a debt consolidation is an efficient tool, which can help you in repairing your credit.

Debt consolidation, as the name implies, consolidates all your debts into just one loan. This means that if you have outstanding debts from various creditors, you can secure a loan from just one company and use the loan amount to pay your outstanding debts. You will only make your payments on a single loan and a single creditor/company.

Through debt consolidation, you will be able to have flexibility when your debts are already unmanageable. While you would still owe the same amount of money, debt consolidation allows you to secure a loan over the long term to lower your monthly payments.

Furthermore, debt consolidation will enable you to improve your relationship with your creditors and paves the way for repairing your credit. Through debt consolidation, your creditors will report to credit bureaus that your debts are already cleared up; thus, the credit repair process can start quickly.

Ultimately, debt consolidation changes your status with your creditors in a quick manner. It stops the damage to your financial situation before it gets worse.

You can be on good terms with just a single creditor as compared to being on bad terms with multiple ones. Besides, debt consolidation allows you to breathe before engaging in credit repair.

WHAT IS IN SECTION 609, YOU HAVE THE RIGHT TO REQUEST

This works by first disputing with the credit report authorities legitimately. Each credit authority has a connection to discuss any of your credit things so you can do this on the web if you wish, or you can submit one recorded as a hard copy by sending them a letter.

Occasionally, a credit report office may evacuate after your first question or dispute. Often, however, you will be required to catch up with further documentation. For instance, if a report contains an equalization mistake, you may need to send receipts or other verification that shows why you trust it is off base.

THE CREDIT DEPARTMENTS' DUTY

A significant part of the duty regarding exact announcing falls on the credit report authorities. That is the reason why the questioning procedure begins with them. As indicated by the FCRA, credit report organizations are required to remember just exact and unquestionable data for your credit report. This implies that if the credit agency does not get palatable reactions from your loan bosses, they are committed to expelling any negatives from your credit report.

CHAPTER 7:

Tips and Tricks for Success with the 609

Whether you want to delete just one thing from your record or you are looking to delete a lot of different things at the same time, you want to make sure that your 609 Letter is taken care of and ready to go. There are a lot of parts that you need to go through to get this done, but when you look at some of the templates that we have in the next section, you will see that this is not as bad as it may seem.

When you are ready to write out some of the letters you need to send out to the credit agencies, and you are getting all of the documentation ready to go, make sure to follow some of the general advice that we have below:

KEEP ALL OF THE RECORDS

Everything must be recorded on your end. Don't just send out a letter and then assume that it is going to be all good. You never know when things are going to go missing or when you will need to prove your side of things. The more accurate and in-depth records you keep, the better it will be for everyone.

This means that we need to keep track of everything from the moment that we start sending out information and letters to the credit bureaus, until way after they take that information off your credit report. This will help you if anything comes back later on, or you need to make sure that you can prove your side of the story if the credit agency doesn't respond or do what they are supposed to.

KEEP TRACK OF EVERYTHING THAT YOU CAN ALONG THE WAY

You should have all the letters that you send out, both the originals and any follow-ups that you send as well. If the credit agency gets in touch with you, then you should keep the letters they send to you as well as your responses.

You can hold onto all the supporting documents that you send each time as well. The more information that you add to your records about this, the better it will be for getting your way in the process.

ADD IN THE IDENTIFICATION INFORMATION

Before you send out any information or work with Section 609, make sure that you send along with it some identification information. This is going to make sure that the credit agency is going to understand who you are and can prove that they are working with the person who says they own the account or at least own the SSN that goes with all that information on the credit report.

There are a lot of different options that you can use for showing your identity, and you should include several of them with your letter to help prove who you are. You would want to work with information like your driver's license, social security numbers, and more to showcase who you are and why you need to make changes in the credit report.

CONSIDER BRINGING SOMETHING UP, EVEN IF IT DOESN'T SEEM IMPORTANT

While you are in this process, it is worth bringing up even some of the smaller things that are on your report. Even if these don't seem important at the time and they are not the main thing you want to focus your attention on, you should add in as many details and as many disputes that are legitimate as possible while you are writing the letter.

You never know what you would be able to get erased off the credit report, and how much of a difference that is going to make to your credit score along the way. Even if the item seems small, you should consider adding it to the dispute.

Sometimes, the time limit will go on too long, and the agency will not respond. If this happens, all the items, whether they are big or small, will need to be taken out of the report. You will find that even a few small things can add up to be big things in the long run.

Even if the credit agency won't erase all of the little things, it doesn't take much of a difference along the way in terms of the time that you take to get it all done.

DO NOT CONTACT THE FTC

One thing that a lot of people are going to try is to contact the FTC and other agencies in the hope of getting things fixed. They may hope that because there is something wrong with the credit report, the FTC will be able to help them take care of this. Sometimes they get mad and want to get the agency in trouble for falsely adding things to their reports, and other times, they may just not know who they are supposed to contact.

However, this is not going to do you any good. If you contact the FTC, they are not going to be able to provide you with the assistance that you need. Their stance is that they are not going to get in between you and the credit agency at all, and all you will get back is a form letter stating these facts. Since you have other options at your disposal to work with, you do not need to work with the FTC.

When you want to get something on your credit report fixed and all better, then it is important not to waste time with the FTC and instead go straight to the credit agencies. You can send the same letter and the same information to each one, and they are the ones who will be able to help get things done. If you follow the rules that we are using here, and some of the other steps that we talked about in this section, you will be able to get your credit report taken care of.

SEND A LETTER TO EACH CREDIT AGENCY

One thing that we need to remember here is that we have to go through the process of sending out one of these Section 609 letters to each credit agency that we want to get to remove the items. The credit agencies are not going to talk to one another about this. If you send out a letter to Transunion, but not to one of the others, then Transunion may take it off your report, but none of the others would do this for you.

You must be responsible for sending a letter to all three of the reporting agencies if you would like to get that debt taken out of all of your reports. You should automatically send this information to all three right from the start, so make sure to get copies of all the information so that you are ready to go and handle all of that at once as well.

You can include the same information in each of the letters that you send out. And you can even send out the same letter, just make sure to change the company and department name that you are using on each one. Then include the same proofs of your identity, the credit reports, and more, for each one to get the ball rolling.

MENTION SECTION 609 IN THE LETTER

There are a few different things that we need to remember when it comes to writing out our form letters. We need to include our name and some of the information about who we are and where we live. We need to include information about the debts and accounts that we would like to dispute along the way, including a credit report to show what accounts we're talking about. And then we need to make sure that we, at some point, mention Section 609 in the letter.

This is going to be useful in several aspects. First, it is going to show the credit agency that you know what you are talking about. There are a lot of people out there who would like to fix their credit scores, but they don't understand the laws, or they are trying to sneak past things. The credit agencies are going to notice these individuals easily and will not want to work with them at all.

However, when you go through and mention Section 609 in your letter like we have talked about so far in this guidebook, then you will find that it is much easier for you to grab their attention. You have done your research, you know what your rights are, and you are ready to take them on to get the credit report taken care of. The credit agencies are going to notice and respect this, and that will make it more likely that they will listen to you and send out the information that you need or erase the information that should not be there.

MENTION THE 30-DAY LIMIT

In addition to making sure that you mention something about Section 609 in the letter you send out, you also need to make sure that you mention the 30 days that the agency gets to respond to you. This not only helps to show that you have a good idea of what you are talking about but will also make it easier for you to remind the credit agency about this right that you have with Section 609.

The letters that we have below are examples of how you can write these out in your form letter. Make sure to mention that you expect the credit agency to respond and work with that time limit to get things taken care of. If you do this, then it is a lot harder for them to come back without knowing about the time limit, and it will set out the same expectations that everyone on both sides needs to follow.

USE ONE OF THE TEMPLATES, SO YOU KNOW WHERE TO START

Making sure that you have all the right parts show up in your letter is going to be a challenge. You want to make sure that you write it out in the right manner, that you mention the right parts about Section 609, and you want to make sure that you sound like you know what you are talking about along the way.

The good news is that we have provided some templates that you can use to take care of this process. There are several Section 609 templates that you can work with at the end of this guidebook, and they will be able to provide you with the right way to word your letters to get them noticed. They will mention Section 609, the FCRA, and even the 30-day notice that is important so that you can write out a letter that is going to get noticed and can help you clean up your credit report.

SEND A FOLLOW-UP LETTER

We may think that all of the work is done, and we won't have to do anything else after we send off the initial letter to all three credit agencies, but unfortunately, there are a few other steps that we need to complete. Once you are certain that the 30 days have passed and you have given the company enough time to respond to what you sent in, it is time to send in the follow-up letter telling them that it is now their responsibility to remove that information from your credit report.

We are going to provide you with a good template that you can use at the end of this guidebook for the follow-up letter, but it will basically tell the agency that you sent in information about the different disputes you had on your credit report, and since they have not replied in the timely manner given by the FRCA in Section 609, it is now time for them to remove those items from your credit report.

These letters can be short, depending on the length of your original dispute, and will not have a lot in them. They will summarize some of the information that you sent out to them a month ago, and then reiterate what your rights are under Section 609 and what you expect the credit agency to do now that the right amount of time has passed.

There are a lot of misconceptions out there when it comes to working with the Section 609 letter, and getting it right is going to make the difference between whether or not you can get the credit agency to do what you would like, which would then increase your credit score.

CHAPTER 8:

609 Letter Templates You Need

LETTER #1 (INITIAL LETTER TO CREDIT BUREAU DISPUTING ITEMS)

{Name of bureau}

{Address}

{Date}

{Name on account}

{Report number}

To whom it may concern:

On {date of credit report} I received a copy of my credit report, which contains errors that are damaging to my credit score. I am requesting the following items be completely investigated as each account contains several mistakes.

{Creditor 1 / Account number}

{Creditor 2 / Account number}

{Creditor 3 / Account number}

Thank you in advance for your time. I understand that you need to check with the original creditors on these accounts and that you will make sure every detail is accurate. I also understand that under the Fair Credit Reporting Act you will need to complete your investigation within 30 days of receiving this letter. Once you are finished with your investigation, please send me a copy of my new credit report showing the changes. I look forward to hearing from you as I am actively looking for a new job and wouldn't want these mistakes on my credit report to stand in my way.

Sincerely,

{Your signature}

{Your printed name}

{Your address}

{Your phone number}

{Your social security number}

Include a copy of the credit report showing which accounts you are disputing

LETTER #2 (WHEN YOU DON'T GET A RESPONSE FROM LETTER #1)

{Name of bureau}

{Address}

{Date}

{Name on account}

{Report number}

To whom it may concern:

On {date of your first letter} I sent you a letter asking you to investigate several mistakes on my credit report. I've included a copy of my first letter and a copy of the report with the mistakes circled. The Fair Credit Reporting Act says I should only have to wait 30 days for the investigation to be finished. It has been more than 30 days and I still have not heard anything.

I'm guessing that since you have not responded that you were not able to verify the information on the mistaken accounts. Since it has been more than 30 days, please remove the mistakes from my credit report and send me a copy of my updated credit report. Also, as required by law, please send an updated copy of my credit report to anyone who requested a copy of my credit file in the past six months.

I look forward to hearing from you as I am actively looking for a new job and wouldn't want these mistakes on my credit report to stand in my way.

Sincerely,

{Your signature}

{Your printed name}

{Your address}

{Your phone number}

{Your social security number}

Include a copy of the credit report showing which accounts you are disputing

Include a copy of your original letter

Include a copy of the registered letter receipts showing the date they received your original letter

LETTER #3 (REQUEST FOR REMOVAL OF NEGATIVE ITEMS FROM THE ORIGINAL CREDITOR)

{Name of creditor}

{Address}

{Date}

{Name on account}

To whom it may concern:

On {date of credit report} I received a copy of my credit report which contains errors that are damaging to my credit score. I am requesting the following items be completely investigated as each account contains several mistakes.

{Description of item(s) you are disputing/account number(s)}

I have included a copy of the credit report and have highlighted the account(s) in question.

Thank you in advance for your time. I understand that you need to check on these accounts and that you will make sure every detail is accurate. I also understand that under the Fair Credit Reporting Act you will need to complete your investigation within 30 days of receiving this letter. Once you are finished with your investigation, please alert all major credit bureaus where you have previously reported my information. Also, please send me a letter confirming the changes.

I look forward to hearing from you as I am actively looking for a new job and wouldn't want these mistakes on my credit report to stand in my way.

Sincerely,

{Your signature}

{Your printed name}

{Your address}

{Your phone number}

{Your social security number}

Include a copy of the credit report showing which accounts you are disputing

LETTER #4 (IF YOU DON'T RECEIVE A RESPONSE FROM LETTER #3)

{Name of creditor}

{Address}

{Date}

{Name on account}

To whom it may concern:

On {date of your first letter} I sent you a letter asking you to investigate several mistakes on my credit report. I've included a copy of my first letter and a copy of the report with the mistakes circled. The Fair Credit Reporting Act says I should only have to wait 30 days for the investigation to be finished. It has been more than 30 days and I still have not heard anything.

I'm guessing that since you have not responded, you were not able to verify the information on the mistaken accounts. Since it has been more than 30 days, please immediately report the updated information to all major credit bureaus so they may update my credit report. Also, please send me a letter confirming these changes to the way you report my account.

I look forward to hearing from you as I am actively looking for a new job and wouldn't want these mistakes on my credit report to stand in my way.

Sincerely,

{Your signature}

{Your printed name}

{Your address}

{Your phone number}

{Your social security number}

Include a copy of the credit report showing which accounts you are disputing

Include a copy of your original letter

Include a copy of the registered letter receipts showing the date they received your original letter

LETTER #5 (IF THE CREDIT BUREAU DOESN'T REMOVE NEGATIVE ITEMS DISPUTED)

{Name of credit bureau}

{Address}

{Date}

{Name on account}

{Report number}

To whom it may concern:

On {date of your first letter} I sent you a letter asking you to investigate several mistakes on my credit report. I've included a copy of my first letter and a copy of the report with the mistakes circled. According to your response, you have chosen to leave these negative items on my credit report adding insult to injury. The items in question are:

{Creditor 1 / Account number}

{Creditor 2 / Account number}

{Creditor 3 / Account number}

I find it completely unacceptable that you and the creditor refuse to investigate my dispute properly. Your refusal to follow the Fair Credit Reporting Act is causing me untold stress and anxiety. Since you won't follow through, I want to know exactly how you investigated each account. Therefore, I would like the name, title, and contact information for the person at the creditor with whom you did the investigation. This will allow me to personally follow up with the creditor and find out why they are choosing to report these mistakes on my credit, month after month.

I know I am only one person among thousands or more that you have to look after, but to me, this is both personally damaging and humiliating. You may not understand it and you don't have to—all I'm asking is that when people look at my credit file, they see the most accurate information and that's not what's happening.

Please provide me with the requested information right away so I can finally put this nightmare behind me.

I look forward to hearing from you as I am actively looking for a new job and wouldn't want these mistakes on my credit report to stand in my way.

Sincerely,

{Your signature}

{Your printed name}

{Your address}

{Your phone number}

{Your social security number}

Include a copy of the credit report showing which accounts you are disputing

Include a copy of your original letter

Include a copy of the bureau's response showing no changes to your credit

CHAPTER 9:

How to Proceed
With The Letters

Now that we know a little bit more about Section 609 and how we can use this for some of our own needs when it is time to handle our credit report and get the different parts to increase, it is time to look at how we can proceed with these letters. In the following section, we are going to take a look at the steps that you can utilize to write out one of these Section 609 letters. But then it is time to figure out what we want to do with them when the letter is written. There are a few different ways that we can make sure these letters get back to the right parties, and all of them are listed below:

EMAILS

Our world seems to run online and using this we can find ways to work on our credit scores. Not having to waste a lot of time copying things or worrying about the paper trails can seem like a great idea, and in some cases, we may find that sending in our 609 letters through email is going to be the best situation for our needs.

Before you do this, though, make sure that you take the time to do the proper research. You want the forms to end up in the right locations, rather than getting sent to the wrong departments and not doing anything for you in the process. Most of the time there will be listings for the various departments that you want to handle and work with for each credit agency, so take a look at those.

Again, when you are ready, you need to have as many details as possible ready to go for this. Just sending in a few lines about the process and thinking that will get things done is foolish. Write out a letter just like you would if you planned to send these by mail and use that as the main body of your email. Mention Section 609 and some of the disputes that you want to bring up.

In addition to this, you need to take some time adding in the other details. Attach some ways to prove your identity to the email, along with a copy of the credit report that has been highlighted to show what is going on and what you would like to dispute. Add in any of the other documentation that is needed to help support your case and have it as clean and organized as possible to make sure the right people can find it and will utilize this information to help you out.

DOING IT ALL ONLINE

Many of the credit agencies have made it easier to go through and work on some of these claims online. This helps you out because you will not need to go through and print it all or worry about finding the paperwork and printing a bunch of things. Also, if you are already on your credit report, your identification has been taken care of.

Since so many people are online these days, doing this right from the credit report is a simple and easy process to work with, and you will catch onto it quickly. Don't take the easy way out of this. If you just click on the part that you think is wrong and submit a claim on it, it won't be enough. There won't be any reference back to Section 609, and you will not be able to get them to follow the rules that come with Section 609 necessarily.

This is where being detailed is going to be useful in the long run. When you do submit one of these claims online, make sure that you write a note with it to talk about Section 609, specifically the part of 609 that you want to reference in this dispute.

You can usually attach other forms to document who you are, and why you think the errors need to be dropped.

Treat this just like you would if you tried to mail the information to the credit agency. The more details that you can include in this, the better. This will help to build up your case and can make it harder for those items to stay on your credit report for a long time. Make sure to mention the 30-day time limit as well.

TELEPHONE

A telephone is one method that you can use, but it is not usually the right one for this kind of process. For example, how easy is it going to be to show the credit agency what your driver's license looks like? You can repeat the number over if you would like, but this process is still a bit more laborious than some of the others and doesn't always work as well as we hope it would.

However, this is an option that we can use to reach the credit agencies, and for some people who are not sure of what their rights are, or would rather talk directly to the individuals in charge about this issue, the telephone can be the right option. Make sure that you have a copy of your credit report in front of you when you start and having some other identification information and more. This will ensure that you are prepared when someone comes on the line to speak with you.

Just like we will show when working on our letter templates, later on, we need to make sure that we speak about the issue at hand, explain our rights, and go through the information on Section 609. There is the possibility that the other side is going to have some questions for you, and they will at least want to go through and verify your identity to make sure they are ready to go. But the same rules apply here, and if you don't get a response within 30 days of that phone call, then the information should be erased.

Keep a record of what is discussed in that conversation, who you talked to during that time, what time and date it was, and so on. This will make it easier to get someone to respond to you and can help us get this to work in our favor. Also, remember that you will need to repeat these phone calls to all three credit bureaus to get your information cleared on all of them.

MAIL

Another option that you can work with is mail. This is usually a good method to use because it allows you a way to send in all of the information at once. Since you probably already have a physical copy of your SSN, driver's license, credit report, and more, you can get copies of these made pretty quickly, and then send them along with the Section 609 letter. This method also allows us a way to go through and circle or highlight the parts of our credit report that we want to point out to the credit reporting agency.

This method is quick and efficient and will make sure that the information gets to the right party. You can try some of the other options, but sometimes this brings up issues like your information getting lost in the spam folder or getting sent to the wrong part. Mails can take some of that out of the way and will ensure that everything gets to the right location at the right time.

CERTIFIED MAIL

For the most part, you are going to find that working with a certified mail is going to be one of the best options that you can choose. This will ensure that the letter gets to the right place and can tell you for certain when the 30-day countdown is going to begin.

If you send this by regular mail, you have to make some guesses on when the letter will arrive at the end address that you want, and sometimes you will be wrong. If there is a delay in the mailing and it gets there too late, then you may start your 30 days too early. On the other hand, if you assume it is going to take so many days and it takes less, you may wait around too long and miss your chance to take this loophole and use it to your advantage.

A certified mail can fix this issue. When the credit agency receives the letter, you will get a receipt about that exact date and even the time. This is going to make it so much easier for you since you can add these to your records. There is no guessing along the way, and you can be sure that this particular loophole is going to work to your advantage.

Another benefit that comes with certified mail is that you make sure that it gets to its location. If you never get a receipt back or get something back that says the letter was rejected or not left at the right place, then you will know about this ahead of time. On the other hand, if it does get to its location, you will know this and have proof of it for later use.

Sometimes things get lost, but you want to be on the winning side of that one. If the credit agency says that they did not receive the letter, you will have proof that you sent it and that someone within the business received it and signed for it. Whether the company lost it along the way, or they are trying to be nefarious and not fix the issue for you, the certified mail will help you get it all to work for you.

When it comes to worrying about those 30 days and how it will affect you, having it all in writing with receipts to show what you have done can take out some of the guesswork in the process. This will ensure that you are going to get things to work for you if the 30 days have come and gone, and no one will be able to come back and say that you didn't follow the right procedures.

As we can see, there are a few different options that we can use when it comes to sending out our Section 609 letters.

CHAPTER 10:

How Can I Work With 609 To File A Dispute?

HOW TO FILE A DISPUTE WITH SECTION 609

It is important to note that there are several template letters for Section 609. What this means is that you can easily download and use one of these templates yourself. While you usually must pay for them, there are some which are free. Of course, you will want to remember to include your information in the letter before you send it.

You will want to make sure everything is done correctly, as this will make it more likely that the information will come off, and no one will place it back on your report again.

1. Find a dispute letter through googling "Section 609 dispute letter". While you might be able to find a free download, for some, you will be able to copy and paste into Microsoft Word or onto a Google Doc.

2. Make the necessary changes to the letter. This will include changing the name and address. You will also want to make sure your phone number is included. Sometimes people include their email address, but this is not necessary. It is always safer to only include your home address or P.O. Box information. You will also want to make sure to edit the whole letter if something does not match up to what you want to say in your message, such as what you are trying to dispute on your credit report. These letters are quite generic, which means you need to add in information related to you.

3. You want to make sure that all the account information you want to be taken off your credit report is handwritten. You also want to make sure you use blue ink rather than black. On top of this, you do not need to worry about being too neat, but you want to make sure they can read the letters and numbers correctly. This is an essential part of filing your dispute letter because handwritten ones in blue ink will not be pushed through their automated system.

They have an automatic mode that will read the letter for them and punch in the account number you use. They will then send you a generic message that states these accounts are now off your credit report, which does not mean that it happened. When you write the information down, a person needs to read it and will then take care of it. Of course, this does not mean that you will not be pushed aside as this can, unfortunately, happen with any letters.

4. You want to make sure that you prove who you are with your letters. While this is never an easy thing to do, you must send a copy of your social security card and your driver's license, or they will shred your letter. You also need to make sure that you get each of your messages notarized. You can typically do this by visiting your county's courthouse.

5. You can send as many letters as you need to; however, keep in mind that the creditor typically will not make you submit more than four. This is because when you threaten to take them to court in the third letter, they will realize that your accounts and demands are just not worth it. First, you could damage their reputation, and secondly, you will cost them more money by doing that compared to only taking the information off your credit report.

6. You will want to make sure that you keep all correspondence they send you. This will come in handy when they try to make you send more information or keep telling you that they cannot

do anything. You must not give up. Many people struggle to get them to pay attention because that is just how the system works. Therefore, you need to make sure that you do not listen to their quick automatic reply that your information is of your credit report. You also want to make sure to wait at least three months and then re-run your credit report to make sure the wrong information has been removed. Keep track of every time you need to re-run your credit report as you can use this as proof if they continue to send you a letter stating the information is off of your credit report.

It is important to note that you can now file a dispute letter online with all three credit bureaus. However, this is a new system, which means that it does come with more problems than sending one through the mail. While it is ultimately your choice whether you use a form to file your 609 dispute or send a letter, you always want to make sure you keep copies and continue to track them, even if you don't hear from the credit bureau after a couple of months. It will never hurt to send them a second letter or even a third.

THE NECESSARY DOCUMENTS BEFORE SENDING THE LETTER

One wellspring of income for them originates from selling the information on our credit reports to different lenders, managers, insurance agencies, credit card organizations, and those you approve of to see your credit information. In addition to the fact that they provide raw data, they likewise sell them using various methods for examining the data to decide the risk of stretching out credit to us. In addition to trading our information to lenders, they likewise sell our data to us. Credit scores, credit observing administrations, extortion security, and wholesale fraud prevention - interestingly enough, this region has quickly gotten perhaps the most significant wellspring of income. Furthermore, those pre-endorsed offers in our letter drop each week or garbage mail? That is right; they got our information from the credit bureaus as well. Organizations buy into assistance provided by the three credit bureaus that sell a rundown of consumer's credit information that fits pre-decided criteria.

Presently, as opposed to prevalent thinking, credit bureaus do not have any contribution. However, by utilizing the entirety of the set information on your credit report (personal information, payment history, and credit propensities) and FICO's technique for scoring that data, they tell them how creditworthy you are.

WHERE TO SEND YOUR 609 LETTERS?

Credit bureaus collect information from various sources following consumer information. The activity is done for multiple reasons and includes data from singular consumers.

Included is the information concerning a person's charge payments and their getting. Utilized for evaluating creditworthiness, the info provides lenders with an outline of your accounts if a loan repayment is required. The interest rates charged on loans are additionally worked out concerning the kind of credit score shown by your experience. It is like this, not a uniform procedure, and your credit report is a vital instrument that affects future loans.

Based on risk-based valuing, it pegs various risks on the multiple customers in this manner, deciding the cost you will acquire as a borrower. Done as a credit rating, it is assistance provided to various interested parties in the public. Terrible credit histories are affected for the most part by settled court commitments, which mark you for high-interest rates every year. Duty liens and bankruptcies, for example, shut you out of the conventional credit lines and may require a great deal of arrangement for any loan to be offered by the bank.

Bureaus collect and examine credit information, including financial data, personal information, and elective data. Various sources give this generally marked data furnishers. These have an exceptional association with the credit bureaus. An average gathering of data furnishers would comprise of creditors, lenders, utilities, and debt collection agencies. Pretty much any association which has had payment involvement in the consumer is qualified, including courts.

Any data collected for this situation is provided to the credit bureaus for grouping. When it is accumulated, the data is placed into specific repositories and files claimed by the bureau. The information is made accessible to customers upon request. The idea of such information is necessary for lenders and managers.

The information is in this manner material in various conditions; credit evaluation and business thoughts are simply part of these. The consumer may likewise require the data to check their score, and the home proprietor may need to check their inhabitant's report before renting an apartment. Since borrowers saturate the market, the ratings will, in general, be robotic. A straightforward examination would deal with this by giving the client a calculation for rapid appraisal and checking your score once every other year to deal with errors in your report.

Individuals from the public are qualified for one free credit report from every one of the significant bureaus. Business reports, for example, Paid, might be gotten on request and are chargeable. Lawful expressions for the credit bureaus incorporate Credit Report Agency or CRA in the U.S. This is organized in the Fair Credit Report Act or FCTA. Other government rules associated with the assurance of the consumer incorporate the Fair and Accurate Credit Transaction Act, Fair Credit Billing Act, and Regulation B.

Statutory bodies have additionally been made for the regulation of the credit bureaus. The Fair-Trade Commission serves as a controller for the consumer credit report agencies. At the same time, the Office of the Comptroller of Currency fills in as a manager of all banks going about as furnishers.

TIPS FOR LETTER WRITING

If you send a credit claim letter to a credit office, you first need to locate your credit report — this can be a bigger task than it seems, particularly since the credit office in question may have reports about almost everybody in the world reporting on it. You will need to provide detail on the mistake after you have found the submission, as well as a clarification as to why you are disputing the object. Eventually, the payment claim letter should include a request to remove the object from the credit report to the credit bureau.

It should have what it needs to decide on your case by providing the bureau with the necessary information.

Here's what to include:

- Updated date
- The particulars (name, contact information, date of birth, and account number)
- Contact information for the Credit office

- A brief description of the mistake (no need for a long and complicated tale to regale them)
- Any documentation you might have that can help prove your point, such as payment records or court documents (be sure to mention in the letter why you submitted them)
- Notes on what you want the credit office to do (re-examine and delete the element from your report)
- A duplicate of the credit report labeled with a mistake
- A scanned copy of your Government ID (such as your driver's license) and a bill or other paper showing your identity

Here are just a few samples of arguable products:

- Collections
- Late payments
- Bankruptcies not stopped until 7 to 10 years
- Pre-closures not lifted until seven years

609 letters are a perfect place to theoretically clear out a few derogatory things that you were not able to delete earlier from your credit report. Even though these are your items, creditors must register them properly and be ready to show it.

Remember that traditional disputes over credit reporting are great, to begin with since you may initially find a few inaccuracies that require to be addressed. Yet another tool in the arsenal are these 609 letters for you to get a better score.

Where to send your credit dispute letter?

Given below are the addresses for the three major credit bureaus.

Experian: - Dispute Department, Post Office Box 9701, Allen, TX 75013

Equifax: - Post Office Box 7404256, Atlanta, G a 30374-0256

TransUnion: - Consumer Solutions, Post Office Box 2000, Chester, P A 19022-2000

Ensure that you keep copies of any records you send to the credit bureaus.

CHAPTER 11:

Step-by-step Guide to Open A Dispute

In 2013, a report by the Federal Trade Commission evaluated that one out of every five people has an inaccurate credit report. On a national scale, that translates to upwards of 42 million missteps. If you wish to remove negative items from your credit reports, you'll have to pursue the dispute goals request process. Requests are made in a formal composed process, in which you will submit letters to the CRAs or creditors expressing which negative items you wish to have removed from your credit reports. From the time of the receipt of the letters, the CRAs have 30 days to make a move. If you find wrong information, you'll pursue a similar process, either requesting an expulsion of the thing (e.g., a collection that isn't yours) or a redress (e.g., a request that late payment is set right).

You may have gotten dispute letterforms with your credit reports. For instance, here a sample dispute goals letter from TransUnion can be found on its website and at tccbonline.com. I've read that during the dispute process, you ought to provide as meager information as conceivable concerning your personal and account information—you shouldn't reference the credit report ID or enclose a duplicate of the CRAs' credit report because thusly, you are just encouraging the reinvestigation process timeline. Driving the CRAs to begin from scratch with no information makes the multi-day check tick faster in support of you, yet it's up to you. I've been fruitful at evacuations utilizing the two strategies.

Remember to stay sorted out during this process. You'll need to keep tabs on your development by keeping a worksheet of the tradelines being disputed, just as the dates when letters are sent. Keep duplicates of everything, and never send in unique duplicates of anything. From the time requests are made, the CRAs are required to react or remove negative and inaccurate information within 30 days.

REINVESTIGATION AND RE-VERIFICATION

The proper terms to request that negative items be removed from credit files are reinvestigation and re-verification; however, these might be misnomers. These are terms utilized distinctly by the CRAs and those in the credit reporting ventures. They are equivalent to a standard examination and verification, however since credit reporting agencies believe that any accumulating report is an examination, they along the lines allude to the process of verifying that data as a reinvestigation.

TARGET ADVERSE AND NEGATIVE ITEMS

While the laws differ from state to state concerning legal time limit on credit report items, for some states most unfriendly information concerning bankruptcies, collections, charge liens, decisions, some polite suits, and some kid bolsters debts are on file for seven years, hard inquiries stay on credit records for two years. All things considered, many have been fruitful at removing negative information from showing up at all on their credit reports, regardless of whether it was theirs.

If you find any inaccurate thing, dispute the information (if this is your course), since it costs nothing. There's constantly a chance that questioning sections can work, as indicated by Dana Neal in Best Credit. Sometimes, either due to a broken record-keeping or noncontact by a unique creditor or collection agency, the CRAs can't verify antagonistic items inside the allowed 30-day time frame; hence, naturally, they should remove them. This dispute process is the starting point to removing negative information, and many will find that they can do so effectively, utilizing the sample letters in this part, by having the CRAs remove the accompanying items from their credit report:

- **Bankruptcies**

If you are attempting to remove a bankruptcy before the end of the standard seven-year reporting period, you'll have a superior shot after at any rate two years from discharge, just after you've disputed and removed all debts that have a status showing they were incorporated under bankruptcy on the credit report.

- **Collections**

If the bureau can't verify that the collection is genuine inside the reinvestigation time frame set out by the FCRA (30 days), at that point, the law requires that it be removed from your report. Collections are regularly reported by administration bureaus, which are famous for committing errors, including translating SSNs inaccurately; if the CRAs can provide verification documentation, guarantee that it has recorded all information accurately since any errors are causes for cancellation.

- Judgment

Attempt to dispute these, else you may need to arrange a settlement with the offended party.

A paid judgment is far superior on a credit record than an unpaid one.

- Tax Liens

While you might be fruitful in having a tax lien removed from your credit report with a standard dispute process if you made good on the regulatory obligation lien in full and it was under $25,000, at that point late news demonstrates that the IRS might be pleased to remove this item from your credit report.

You may not charge so well if the tax lien is more noteworthy than this amount, and it is unpaid.

- Inquiries

Hard inquiries ding your credit score. Dispute them to have them removed, particularly if you don't recognize them.

Remember that rate shopping, stating it in case you're attempting to get preapproved with a mortgage lender for another home, inside a 30-day timeframe won't ding your credit. Prescreened offers likewise won't ding your scores, as these are viewed as delicate pulls.

TARGET ERRONEOUS ITEMS

In addition to questioning antagonistic items, you'll need to dispute negative items that aren't yours by any means. Whenever the situation allows, you'll need to provide proof, just if it will address the item. Try not to mistake this for questioning antagonistic information, which concerns the whole erasure of a negative item. For instance, if you have a credit card tradeline showing a late payment that you need to dispute, you wouldn't have any desire to have the whole tradeline removed from your report, as this is unreasonable; rather you'd simply need the late payment amended if you have evidence of timely payment.

A DISPUTE IN WRITING, NOT ONLINE

It's ideal to request your free yearly credit reports recorded as a hard copy to be delivered via mail from every one of the CRAs. In addition to the fact that this gives you a total picture of what every bureau has on file for you, yet it likewise prevents you from being dependent upon any limitations of obligation and mediation understandings that you should consent to while obtaining online reports.

Most online dispute forms give you enough room to express your dispute; however, it doesn't give you enough room to back it up. Online disputes are likewise not set up to accept additional evidence, for example, a duplicate of your Social

Security card or a check, say specialists—and those bits of evidence can be important later if you do need to go to court to prove that a credit reporting agency isn't amending a genuine mix-up. Also, numerous online dispute forms contain mediation conditions, which can undermine your consumer rights.

Type up at that point, mail your dispute

That way, you can incorporate a lot of information and evidence as you have to clarify your case. Likewise, if you do end up in court, you'll have the option to prove to the judge allocated to your case, that you gave the credit bureaus enough information to explore your dispute properly.

Send in your dispute letters via mail

Better, send them by affirmed mail, or with delivery affirmation, so you can guarantee your archives were gotten. Keep duplicates of your dispute letter and all nooks. Compose the affirmed mail number on each letter so you can without much of a stretch match the ensured letter affirmation with the first dispute.

If you have different items to dispute, don't attempt to dispute every one of them together. Contesting single items or close to two items one after another is the best practice, since, for instance, dispute letters that contain up to eight disputes at a solitary time may raise warnings and caution the CRAs that you are in an ultra-credit-cleanup mode, so don't catch their attention. Rather, utilize the appropriate dispute template letter for close to two errors one after another. For additional disputes, mail those in separately on separate dispute letters. The probability of showing signs of improvement increases if the CRAs handle your disputes each in turn.

Make sure that if you are questioning a negative item that is showing just on a solitary CRA's report, for instance, an account that is present on your Equifax report and not your Experian report, you send in the dispute letter to the right CRA. While the CRAs aren't committed to advising one another, I've read that they now and again speak with one another regarding inaccurate information to be removed. By and by, you wouldn't have any desire to bring on additional disarray or draw consideration structure from the different CRAs to any information that is not currently there.

SEND YOUR LETTERS TO CRAS AND THE ORIGINAL CREDITOR

You can likewise log complaints with the Consumer Financial Protection Bureau. After we forward your complaint, the organization has 15 days to respond to you and the CFPB. Organizations are required to close everything except the most entangled complaints within 60 days. You'll have the option to review the reaction and give us criticism.

If we locate that another agency would be better ready to help, we will advance your complaint and let you know. We likewise share complaint data with state and government agencies who supervise financial items and administrations, and we distribute a database of non-personal complaint information, so the public recognizes what kinds of complaints we get and how organizations respond.

PURSUE THE FORMULA

The best dispute letters are frequently the most effortless to read. Don't attempt to impel lawful contentions or utilize confounding, counterfeit legalese, or other extravagant expressions and words. Numerous letters that have been posted online as samples don't make sense and are ineffective and will accomplish nothing for you. Rather, a concise, dispute letter that states considerately in plain English what the blunder is and what you need to be done about it is ideal. You should be clear about what you're contesting. "The account was rarely mine," or "The payment was rarely late," is not necessary. The letter must come straightforwardly from you, the consumer, to trigger credit bureau commitments for examination.

CHAPTER 12:

What the Credit Bureaus And Lawyers Don't Want You To Know

L isted herein are what credit repair companies don't want you to know and some myths about Credit.

IT WILL REMAIN ON YOUR CREDIT REPORT FOR YEARS

A bankruptcy filing will remain a permanent stain on your credit report for seven to ten years, which may have a devastating effect on your potential credit-obtaining ability.

BANKRUPTCY FILING BECOMES PUBLIC DOMAIN

Bankruptcy is a legal process that ensures it becomes a public record when you file for bankruptcy.

That means that your name and other personal information will appear in court records accessible to the public (including companies, banks, clients, or even potential employers).

FILING DOESN'T ERASE ALL DEBT

Bankruptcy courts have the power to eliminate certain unsecured debts, such as medical bills and credit card balances, but student debt still has to be repaid in full (unless you enroll in any of the loan forgiveness services of the federal government).

FILING IS EXPENSIVE FOR THOSE WITHOUT MONEY

You are filing for bankruptcy because you don't have enough money to pay for payments and debt mounting.

Rates vary by location, but it can take as long as three or five years to conclude a bankruptcy filing, with attorney fees ranging between $2,200 to $3,200 anywhere.

GOOD LUCK FINDING A DECENT HOME LOAN ANY TIME SOON

The reality that bankruptcy filers face far harder hurdles in securing a mortgage loan hardly comes as a surprise in a banking world where banks are already skittish about loaning money for a home.

It can take a new bankruptcy filer up to four years before they are accepted for another mortgage loan, according to the Home Buying Institute. Even the Federal Housing Administration needs borrowers to wait at least two years before they can qualify for an FHA home loan after they declare bankruptcy.

There are so many different pieces of information floating around about credit, a lot of which are just myths. We live in an age of information but one of the drawbacks of this is that with so much information, it can be hard to weed out the facts from the myths. Adhering to some of these myths can hurt your credit health.

The first myth that I want to talk about is that having good credit means you have unnecessary debt. I cannot stress enough how untrue this is, it just comes down to understanding how it all works and using it to your advantage, and most importantly, using it responsibly. As referenced early on, having no credit is just as bad as having poor credit, and many people fall into this category because they are always taught from a young age that "credit and credit cards are evil" or "people only use credit when they cannot afford something." This line of thinking is outdated and detrimental when you reach a point where you need to utilize credit. Credit is a great tool, but it requires self-control. Credit cards should be treated as debit cards; only pay for what you can afford, and things you were going to buy anyway such as gas and groceries, and then pay them in full every month to build your credit. If you already spend $60 on gas on your debit card every month, putting that same amount on your credit card and then paying it off does not result in you losing any money or going into debt, it only helps you increase your credit score. However, if you get a credit card and start buying things you cannot afford like expensive clothes and jewelry, the blame falls on you for lacking self-control, not on the company that gave you the credit card.

Another common myth, and reason that many people avoid credit cards in particular, is that you have to pay an excessive amount of money in interest. This is a myth because while credit cards do have an interest, it only applies when you carry a balance on your credit card for longer than one month. As I mentioned before, the goal is only to charge what you can afford, and therefore you can pay your card in full every month. By doing this you will only have the positive effect of building your credit and you will never have to pay any interest.

The third myth is that carrying a small balance on your credit card will help your score. This is completely untrue, as this will result in interest payments due to that revolving balance. There is a myth that lenders may close an account if it has not been used for an extended time. However, using the card often and paying it off will prevent this from happening. It will also prevent you from paying any interest at all which makes it the best method to utilize.

One of the factors of your credit score is each hard inquiry and how they will lower your score. This has sparked the myth that every time you check your credit score, your score will suffer. This is true for hard inquiries, but there is also what is known as a soft inquiry. A soft inquiry is typically when you check your credit information via an online service or through your bank for free. You can check your credit information fifty times per day, and you will see no impact on your score because a soft inquiry does not hurt you. Therefore, it is important to keep an eye on your credit regularly as it will not have any consequences. If there are any mistakes on your report that are negatively affecting you, you can catch them quickly and file a dispute to get them removed.

Another popular myth I want to cover is that having too many credit cards is a bad thing. It goes back to self-control and understanding that you should not be spending money you do not have just because you have the credit available to you.

We talked about how credit utilization is a high impact factor in your credit score, so having several credit cards will increase your total available credit line which will in turn boost your credit score. Simply having a larger amount of credit available to you will help you because it shows lenders that you can manage a large amount of money without spending it on things you do not need and cannot afford.

The final myth that you may have heard is that you need a perfect credit score of 850 to get the lowest interest rates when buying a home or car. A score of 850 or anything over 800 is honestly really just good for bragging rights. Generally, a score of 720 and above is what you want to strive for. When you apply for a car loan or a home loan, the interest rate can only be as low as the lender can allow. If the best interest rate they can offer you is around 3%, the person who has a score of 740 will typically get the same benefits as the person who has an 850 score. It is not important to strive for a perfect score, just follow the habits outlined in this book and your score will inevitably rise to high levels.

CHAPTER 13:

Elimination of Requests From the Report

HOW TO REMOVE MISTAKES FROM CREDIT REPORT

Initiate a Dispute Online, By Mail, Or by Phone

You may initiate a dispute about an inaccurate or incomplete item on your credit report online, by telephone, or by email.

Initiating a dispute online is the simplest way. The three national CRAs enable you to dispute information in your credit report using the internet.

You may also initiate a dispute through email. If you prefer not to utilize the internet procedure, you can email in your dispute when you have compiled a listing and have prepared a letter identifying the reasons that support your dispute as well as every correction.

If there are mistakes, information that is outdated, or information in your credit file, you might dispute these things. Send your correspondence for disputing the data provided and keep a copy of your records. Add copies of any documents you have that support your claim, and it even may be helpful to add a copy of your credit report using the items. Make sure to maintain your documents.

You can also initiate a dispute using the telephone. To begin a dispute by telephone, call Report. (See below for directions about the best way to locate the telephone numbers for your CRAs.)

To find contact info for initiating a credit dispute go online. Here is where to search:

Equifax: Proceed to Equifax.com. Click "Dispute something in my Equifax credit report."

Experian: Proceed to Experian.com. Click "Disputes" then "How to Dispute" to find out how you can submit your dispute online, by email, or by telephone.

TransUnion: Proceed to TransUnion.com. Click "Find out how to dispute an item in your credit report." This page will provide you with information about how you can initiate a credit dispute. (Visit the "Credit Disputes FAQs" link to find out how to submit your dispute online, by email, or by telephone.)

WHAT HAPPENS AFTER YOU SUBMIT YOUR DISPUTE

When the CRA receives them, it has to delete them within three business days after getting your dispute or reinvestigate. When the Bureau doesn't delete the data in 3 business days, it needs to:

- Complete its evaluation within 45 days (otherwise, it merely contains 30 days, which is extended up to 45 days if you send the bureau additional pertinent information through the 30-day interval).
- In five business days of getting your dispute, contact the lender reporting the info which you disputed. Review and consider all pertinent information which you submitted and forward this info to the lender that supplied the data, and when any modifications have been made, offer you the outcomes of its reinvestigation in five business days of conclusion.

With regards to frivolous disputes, in many situations, the CRA has a responsibility to explore a product as soon as you dispute it.

This implies that in case you dispute everything or nearly everything from the report – concerning what you think is right or wrong – or you ask for reinvestigation of the identical thing, the credit reporting bureau might not need to research your dispute in any way.

When the CRA Does Not Respond To Your Dispute

If the CRA doesn't respond to your dispute within the time constraints imposed by legislation, you might:

Dispute it

Should you publish the dispute, make sure you offer some new details. It may determine if your dispute is frivolous, without providing any info to the CRA should you dispute the mistake.

Submit a criticism to the CFPB

You could also submit a complaint to the Consumer Financial Protection Bureau (CFPB).

This principal agency manages CRAs, together with a copy of the disputed info you've sent to the CRA.

Speak with a lawyer

If you have exhausted the other alternatives for fixing your credit file, along with the CRA still will not resolve the error or mistakes, think about talking to a consumer law attorney who will help you enforce your rights.

Leave the Mistake on the accounts

Only in instances when you aren't damaging your credit score or will be scheduled to fall off your credit report. You ought to keep reviewing your credit reports if they are serious to avoid these mistakes. If the credit reporting agency is struggling to alter your report and you think the information is incomplete or wrong, you will want to take action. Below are a few suggestions that will assist you with your attempts.

Contact the Creditor Directly

Contact the lender, which supplies the advice and demands that it informs the credit reporting bureau to eliminate the information. You could use inaccurate information. If you have received a letter from the lender that ought to have been deleted from the credit history, you could send a copy to the bureau that made the faulty report. If you contacted the funding, they do not need to manage this dispute unless you supply the information. Since you think the dispute wasn't properly researched, you should increase your complaint until the president or CEO and the provider is likely to reply. If the company can't or won't help you in removing the inaccurate info, call the credit reporting agency. Credit reporting bureaus have fees to manage consumer disputes regarding items in their credit files, which are not eliminated through the standard reinvestigation procedure. (Visit the Equifax, Experian, and TransUnion sites to locate contact info for all these three national credit reporting bureaus.)

Document another Dispute with the Credit Reporting Agency with More Information

If you have information to back up your claim, it is possible to submit a fresh dispute.

Make sure to provide it. Should you dispute by mistake without giving any information to the bureau, it will mean that your dispute is frivolous, so the bureau does not need to make inquiries about the issue.

File a Complaint about the Credit Reporting Agency

You can file a complaint regarding a Credit reporting bureau together with the Consumer Financial Protection Bureau (CFPB). The CFPB will attempt to have a response and will forward your complaint. If CFPB believes another government agency will be able to assist you, it allows you to know and will forward your complaint.

File a Complaint Concerning the Creditor

If the lender that supplied the erroneous or incomplete data fails to revise it or notify the credit reporting service for a correction (or even if it advises the credit reporting bureau of this alteration, but reports the incorrect information again after), you might file a complaint with the Federal Trade Commission (FTC).

On the other hand, if the lender is a big institution, you might file a complaint. The CFPB manages different types of agencies, and that means a complaint can be documented.

If you are not sure which agency to contact, begin with CFPB or even the FTC, which will forward your complaint. Normally, you won't be represented by these government agencies, but they could send an inquiry, and they may take action when there are complaints or proof of wrongdoing.

Complaint to Your State Consumer Protection Agency

Some countries have to credit reporting lenders or bureaus furnishing information.

File a complaint with the attorney general or consumer protection bureau of your state.

Get Your Congressional Representative or Senator

After all, they write the legislation. When there are issues with all the legislation or their enforcement and will be a need to know, your congressperson may telephone FTC or the CFPB and request it to investigate.

Consider Suing the Credit Reporting Agency or Creditor

If you were hurt – state after you asked for corrections – contemplate filing a lawsuit, that the credit reporting bureau continued to provide inaccurate or incomplete information. Under the Fair Credit Reporting Act (FCRA) (15 U.S.C. § 1681 and after), you might sue a credit reporting bureau for negligent or deliberate non-compliance with the legislation over two years once you detect the damaging behavior or over five years following the damaging behavior, whichever is earlier.

Based on the breach, you may have the ability to win punitive damages, statutory damages, damages, court costs, and attorneys' fees. You may also consider using the incorrect information was provided by funding that. However, if you would like to pursue this kind of lawsuit, you will have to speak with an attorney.

Consider Adding an Explanatory Statement for Your Credit Report

You've got the right statement for your credit score. As soon as you submit a statement regarding the dispute using a credit reporting agency, the agency must include your statement or a list of it. It might limit your announcement in case the agency helps you in writing the excuse. There is no time limit, though it is a fantastic idea to maintain the announcement shortly. In this way, the credit reporting agency is inclined to utilize your remark.

Speak to a Lawyer

In case you need help repairing your credit file, think about talking to a consumer protection lawyer. A lawyer can help you enforce your rights from a lender or an agency that violates the FCRA.

CHAPTER 14:

Rebuild Your Credit Score

I mproving your credit score is a time-consuming process. Even with the best methods, tactics, and systems, it takes time to see any improvement. These are the ideas that have a positive impact on your grade. You can choose to do the same because these are just good financial habits anyway.

CALCULATE INCOME

Many credit problems can be avoided with the simple process of having a budget for your income. It is the activity of organizing expenses in the appropriate areas that will give you a good idea of where you need to go, how much disposable income you have, and how much you can pay for the monthly installments.

Once you have a budget, you can start developing records of the expenses you have made. This will help you reduce your costs, prevent you from overspending your finances, and allow you to get out of debt faster.

PAY YOUR BILLS ON TIME

If you want to increase your credit score, it is essential not to add additional negative items to your credit report. Most businesses report late payments that exceed the credit limit, so it makes sense to avoid new negative items appearing on your report. If you have trouble knowing when all the payments are made, you can try to:

- Select a day of the month to pay all bills

- Keep a monthly calendar and record all due dates on invoices

- Pay invoices that arrive by mail as soon as they are received

When you run out of money in your payment account, contact the relevant companies as soon as possible, and request an extension. Also, ask them not to report your late payment on your loan.

SAVE MONEY

Today, the company is full of products and services that offer instant gratification; as a result, people feel that if a product or service doesn't get immediate results, it is somehow inferior or of poor quality. This idea has flooded the lives of people to the point where people no longer save money over a long point to be able to buy items with big bills. Instead, they buy them on credit, and if they have enough credit card space, they feel like they can afford it. That's why people live paycheck to paycheck. We are spending more and more revenue on debt service.

If, on the other hand, you start to practice deferred gratification by saving money over some time for large purchases, you will find that your interest rates will drop, you will pay less for the items you want, and you will have the benefits of savings needed or credit available to maintain your lifestyle in an emergency.

Open a savings account and invest money in it until you save at least two months of income. This will give you a two-month clipboard to troubleshoot or overcome an emergency. Living on paid income is an expensive way of life.

CHECK YOUR CREDIT REPORT ANNUALLY

You have the legal right to receive a free copy of your credit report from the three major credit bureaus every three years.

Use this right and get a free copy every year. Please check for errors as it is estimated that 80% of all credit reports contain errors that affect the overall result. If you discover items that you think are incorrect, you can trigger them, and if the reporting agency does not prove that the report is valid, you should remove it from the report.

Second, a review of your credit report will show your trends in your financial habits. Do you make the same mistake often? Forget your payments? By reviewing the report, you will tell what you are doing that is harming your relationship and enabling you to make positive changes.

GET INVOLVED WITH A LOAN REPAIR COMPANY

Depending on how quickly you need results, how much time you need to spend taking the necessary actions to get results, and your willingness to learn what to do and when you will determine which product or service to use.

Some people say that you can do the same things as credit repair companies and it is true. You have the lawful right to do whatever the credit houses do to improve results. The difference is that they already have. They know which methods work and which have little effect.

No one would suggest that you defend yourself in court, even if you have the same legal rights you would have with a lawyer. However, your chances of success are exponentially higher if you hire a lawyer.

PAY YOUR BILLS ON TIME

Maybe it's a credit card bill or a monthly loan payment, the essential way to improve your credit score is to avoid late fees. If you can't remember when your account expires, configure the system to stay unionized. Create a calendar that tags the days you have to pay. Or consider setting up automatic withdrawals for your accounts. This way, the amount owed will be paid every month on time.

PAY THE DEBT

Sometimes cardholders who are struggling to pay off their debts move from one place to another. Opening new accounts and reassigning balances may not be the best solution. To improve your credit score, you want to pay off all your debts. Make a payment plan to get rid of all balances and limit spending until the debt is gone completely. If you have minimal debt, creditors will see that you can make payments and manage your funds well.

REDUCE THE OPENING OF NEW ACCOUNTS

You may be used to opening new accounts regularly. Lenders sometimes view this practice as a dispute over getting more credit than you can repay. Before opening a new account, assess the benefits you will get from it. It may be better for you to pay off the unpaid debt first and then apply for a new credit or credit card.

STICK TO LOAN CARDS

If you have a little credit rating and want it to go up, you don't have to cut all of your credit cards. Closing too many accounts at once can be bad for you. Your credit history is an essential part of your overall score, so you should stick to a few accounts to maintain a long line of credit.

MANAGE YOUR CREDIT CARDS WISELY

One of the main reasons why consumers have credit problems is financial mismanagement. As you work to add up your credit score, carefully monitor your spending habits. Make small purchases with your credit card and pay for them immediately. Keep track of all your bills and take the time each week to review your finances. If you find it difficult to manage, contact a financial advisor, and seek help.

Typically, the FICO score ranges from 300 to 850. The higher the score, the better. If you make smart financial changes, you can expect your credit rating to improve over time.

A good credit score will open many doors for you in the credit world. You can expect lower interest rates on loans and the ability to apply for credit cards with many benefits. Continue to manage your credit wisely, and you will have plenty of financial opportunities in the future.

REMOVE NEGATIVE ITEMS FROM YOUR CREDIT REPORT

With careful consideration of the details and a well-written controversial letter, you can successfully remove wrong entries from your credit report and improve your score. Check your report for suspicions and write a letter asking the credit reporting companies to confirm it.

NO NEW LOANS

If you want to get the best credit score; you have to learn to practice vigilance. This means that unless it is necessary, you will never apply for a new loan, because every time you put a request in your report and the more inquiries you have, the lower the score will be.

MANAGE CREDIT CARDS RESPONSIBLY

Showing that you can handle credit cards responsibly and paying off your credit can also mean a higher credit score. So, keep 1-2 cards and always pay your loans on time.

KEEP YOUR BALANCE LOW

If your credit card balance goes up, your average score can drop as much as 70 points, so always keep that in mind.

There are many ways to increase your credit score without relying on credit companies. The important thing is to research these available methods as they will help you a lot.

CHAPTER 15:

Credit Protection and Monitoring

WHAT YOU NEED TO KNOW ABOUT CREDIT CARDS

Knowing everything you can about the credit card game is important. Almost everyone has a credit card, but few people know how to use it correctly. Chances are you are reading this book because you have already made financial mistakes and you want to fix them.

Don't Apply for a Credit Card Without Reading the Terms First

When you are choosing a credit card, there is more to it than selecting the design or the credit card issuer. You need to evaluate the card on other factors as well. Consider what kind of card you want. Do you want a rewards credit card, a regular credit card, a student credit card, or a card that you can transfer a balance to? How you are planning on using a credit card is also something that you need to consider. If you are going to be carrying a balance on the card, look for a low-interest rate. Find out what the annual percentage rate (APR) is on the credit card, and also what the grace period is that you can pay your balance in full before you are charged an additional finance charge. Finally, find out what the yearly fees on the card are and what the reward structure is on the card.

Don't Use Credit Cards for Necessities

If you have the money on hand to use for things like clothes, gas, and groceries, do not use your credit cards for these things. Most people find themselves on the road to debt by using their credit in place of cash. If you are using your credit card as a way to build your credit, it can be wise to use it in place of money, as long as you are making sure that you are putting the same amount of money aside from your bank account to put back on your credit card.

If you are using the money on your credit card for groceries and still spending the money that you have in the bank, you are going to find yourself in debt very quickly.

Don't Get into The Habit of Only Making Minimum Payments

By paying only the minimum amount required on an account, you are only putting off the debt that you owe which also increases the amount of interest you are going to accrue on the account. Usually, minimum payments are only the amount of interest gained on the outstanding balance so you won't even be making payments toward the actual principal debt.

By paying as much as possible toward the balance, you are helping to decrease the amount of principal which in turn decreases the amount of interest you will pay in the long run.

Don't Use Credit for Things You Can't Pay For

Don't live above your means. If there is an expensive item you want but don't need, it's important to recognize that if you don't have the money for it now, you probably won't have it anytime soon. Wait until you have the money to pay for your purchases before you purchase them.

However, sometimes you need to make a high-ticket purchase because there is an emergency, for example, your fridge dies, or you need a new furnace.

In an emergency, it would be appropriate to use your credit card as long as you are making it a priority to pay the balance on your credit card back down.

Don't Close a Credit Card Account Without Knowing How It Is Going to Impact Your Credit Score

Closing a credit card account may negatively affect your credit score. Avoid closing accounts with balances or accounts you've had for many years that have made up a great portion of your credit history.

When you look at your credit report, you are going to be able to see how long you have had a credit account open. If you have had your credit card for ten years and it is in good standing, it is not a good idea to close it, especially if all your other credit accounts are newer.

Let Your Creditor Know If You Won't Be Able to Make Your Monthly Payment on Time

Ignoring the situation is not going to make it go away. If you are unable to make a payment on time, contact the company, and discuss available options.

Many times, they will work with you to adjust your due date and waive late fees if you know this will be a one-time problem.

Keep an Eye on Your Utilization

Remember, you want to keep the utilization below 20%. That means that you are going to want to try to keep the amount on your card within 20% of your credit limit. Not only is this going to keep your balance low and more manageable, but it will also help to keep your credit score high.

Ask for a Lower Interest Rate

If you have maintained or improved your credit and begin to receive offers from other institutions offering you a lower rate than you are currently paying, contact your creditors and ask if they will lower your interest rate.

Review Your Credit Card Statement Thoroughly Every Month

Don't assume that everything that is on your credit card statement is accurate. Read through every transaction and ensure that your last payment was applied correctly, that you were charged correctly for all your purchases, and that there are no unauthorized charges on your account. Report unauthorized charges to your credit card company immediately and dispute errors within sixty days of them occurring.

Using a credit card can be the fastest and most effective way for you to build up good credit. However, it can also be the fastest way to ruin your credit. Use the tips above to ensure that you are using your credit card wisely and you will see your credit score begin to climb.

CHAPTER 16:

Maybe You Need A Credit Professional?

CCP
Certified Credit Professional

When you need assistance with getting issues related to your credit straightened out, there are some options available.

IDENTITY THEFT

If your particular case is fraud-related, there are some organizations you can reach out to, including:

- https://www.identitytheft.gov/
- Internet Crime Complaint Center
- https://www.fraud.org/

IDENTITY THEFT RESOURCE CENTER

Contact the credit bureaus and have them place a credit freeze or fraud alert on your credit report.

A three-month fraud alert is fairly simple to have done, but a seven-year fraud alert requires that you file a police report about the identity theft that occurred.

CREDIT COUNSELING

Credit counseling is typically free and available to consumers that would like assistance in getting out of debt.

The financial counseling agencies can give you a suggested budget to work with and a creditor review.

Credit counseling agencies can work with low-income individuals and individuals who can't afford to pay.

Credit counselors can be found at:

- https://www.nfcc.org/ (800) 388-2227
- https://fcaa.org/ (800) 450-1794
- https://www.militaryonesource.mil/ (800) 342-9647 (this option is for military members)

CREDIT REPAIR COMPANIES

If you feel like you have exhausted your free options and are still struggling to repair your credit, credit repair companies offer to improve your credit for a fee.

But it is very important to verify the legitimacy of these companies before doing business with them.

OTHER

- https://careconnectusa.org/

Offers help with collections, student loan relief, childcare assistance, debt relief, free bankruptcy advice, and more.

- https://www.consumerfinance.gov/

Offers answers to hundreds of financial questions.

HOW TO FIND A REPUTABLE CREDIT COUNSELOR

A credit counselor is simply a certified and trained expert in money management. A credit counselor has a great influence on your credit report and can provide you with the specifics that you need to take control of your finances.

Finding a professional credit counselor could serve as the bridge between financial empowerment and wallowing in debt that is worse than where you began.

If you are engrossed with debt, or your credit score is in a ship that is about to sink, and you need to get your financial life back on track – then you need professional help.

Credit counselors help you determine the best options available for you to gain relief from the financial pressure you might be experiencing. There are various ways in which they do this:

- First and foremost, they review your credit report. This is the basic step that must be taken while trying to recover from your present financial chaos.
- They offer numerous probable and applicable solutions to your financial problems; the offered solutions vary from individual to individual.
- They advise you on the best ways to manage your debt.
- They help you develop a plan that is unique to your financial challenges to help you prevent future difficulties.

There are some steps to take while finding a reputable credit counselor.

KNOW WHAT YOU WANT AND HOW TO GET IT

Before reaching out to any credit counseling agency to request the help of a credit counselor, you need to understand your specific needs and how the counselor could be of help. Write out your financial problems and goals, prioritize them before tendering them to the credit counselor. It's of great benefit for you to get a vast counselor with specialized training such as debt settlement and management, students' loan management, bankruptcy counseling among others. There are lots of credit service agencies that can be of service to you at a minimal fee, the U.S. Department of Justice has a special tool that makes it possible to search for those agencies. There are lots of other available agencies and organizations that offer such services.

CHECKING FOR QUALIFICATIONS SHOULD BE YOUR PRIORITY

You need to get registered with agencies and organizations that are affiliated with the Financial Counselling Association of America (FCAA) or the National Foundation for Credit Counselling (NFCC) as they meet standards of certification that ensure distribution of uniform quality. As soon as you can find a credit counseling agency that is trustworthy, the next step is referring to the Better Business Bureau (BBB). This is your first-line defense against fraudulent financial services.

NON-PROFITS CAN BE OF ASSISTANCE

Non-profits can also help you in your time of financial chaos and are preferable compared to profit-making organizations. Council on Accreditation is a popular non-profit organization that approves other social service organizations that demonstrate interest and commitment to help consumers.

A non-profit organization provides unbiased financial assistance to consumers. When you call for a consultation, apart from being free, they also tend to make all your options known to you and also help you pick the best one that fits perfectly for your financial situation.

BE PATIENT

Getting a professional credit counselor is not a decision you want to be hasty about. You need to properly investigate the organization to understand how they work and attend to customers' needs to see if it's going to be in your best interest.

There are also some questions that you need to ask to get the best counselor for you:

- Do you offer information?

Some organizations charge to provide you with the necessary information that will help your financial chaos, avoid such an organization.

- What are your counselor's qualifications?

Ensure that they are certified counselors with experience. Check for their professional background and ensure that the Better Business Bureau (BBB) hasn't filed complaints against your credit counselor.

- What kind of service do you provide?

This is a foremost question that you should ask your counselor before providing detailed information about your financial state. Ensure that you look for organizations that offer a range of services, including debt management classes, savings, bankruptcy, budget counseling, *etc.* Ensure that the option provided for you isn't only a Debt Management Plan (DMP).

- Are you going to sign a Non-Disclosure Agreement (NDA)? What are the assurances that the information you have about me will be kept confidential?
- How much are your fees? Do you have a setup that can allow me to pay up monthly? This is also a consideration that should be properly investigated before selecting a credit counselor.
- What if I don't have enough money to pay for your services? This shouldn't be a constraint for an organization that wants to help, if they are proving reluctant – go somewhere else.

- Will I need to sign any written agreement or contract? If there are any, ensure that you carefully read it, to ensure that all the terms listed are favorable to you.
- Are you a licensed credit counselor? Do you have a license to offer your services in my state of residence?

Conclusion

It can be tough to live without credit in a society where all is dependent on credit. You will not be willing to pay for major investments like a house or college tuition without the opportunity to invest — even without a good credit rating — and you may even think about what you can gain from the wealth-building this will result in. However, credit is not the solution to all your financial problems; you need to invest carefully and selectively use credit to support your financial future, not harm it. Your credit score may be influenced by a variety of variables and while the specific parameters may differ by scoring type, the payment history is usually the most important aspect. Just one missing payment will adversely affect your ranking.

You should now have a better idea of how to repair your credit with or without using Section 609. While many people feel that this is one of the best ways to get rid of your bad credit, there are a lot of situations where writing a dispute letter will not help you gain better credit. For example, if you have missed payments on your credit cards within a certain amount of time. Even if the credit card company states that you didn't pay during the months you did, this is something that won't work in dispute because you have recently missed payments.

When it comes to struggling with credit card debts, the best way to start repairing your credit is to make sure you understand the federal laws associated with credit card debt. Be assured that you have been protected and that the credit card company is not doing anything illegally. If everything is legal, then you simply want to work on paying off your credit card payments.

Section 609 is a great option to work with when it is time to handle getting your credit reports cleared up, and we are going to work with some of the best templates that we can work with to ensure that we can send in the information about the incorrect or invalid parts of our credit reports and get it all to match up and clear out, raising our credit scores in the process. It does take a little time, but with a bit of perseverance and the right wording, you can get it done much faster than what you would be able to do if you just waited for it to all fall off naturally.

While credit repairs may be a simple process, it could take most of your time as well as effort. As you have learned from this book, you need to obtain a copy of your credit report. Remember, you have the right to request your credit history from the concerned credit bureau or reporting agency. You can also download your credit report from the agency's website for a certain fee.

There are three credit reporting agencies from which you can obtain your credit report. These are the Equifax, Experian, and TransUnion. You can also check out their websites and download your credit report from each of them.

Once you have a copy of your credit history, examine it thoroughly. It is best if you compare each item with your stubs of payments and spending. For any inaccuracy, mistake, or discrepancy, make sure to contact the concerned credit bureau and request for an investigation on the item in question. Make sure to request the investigation once you have found out about the inaccuracy so that you can act immediately and proceed to repair your credit. It is also advisable to establish a timeline once you have requested an investigation from the credit bureau. Check with the agency again if they fail to respond within your timeline or 30 days. If the credit agency does not respond within 30 days, request the removal of the item in question from your credit report. Again, it is your right to have it removed due to non-compliance of the agency.

On the other hand, if there is no inaccuracy in your report and you admit that your bad credit situation is your own doing, you should seriously monitor your finances. Make sure to plan your finances. For instance, cut down on unnecessary spending and/or pay your creditor the full amount due. Most creditors provide their customers with additional time to pay up debts;

however, it will only add up to your expenses if you delay your payment.

When you are dealing with a creditor, it is best to let them know that you are serious about repairing your credit. Often, creditors appreciate the effort of their customers in repaying their debts as it saves both time and effort. However, make sure that whatever deal you come up with, you would stick to your word.

The process of credit repair may be a daunting and time-consuming task. However, it is also a circumstance from which you can learn. For instance, you would learn to use your credit wisely once you obtain a good credit rating given that you would not want to go through the entire credit repair process again. You learn how to manage your finances and budget more efficiently than before. You also learn to control your spending urges, specifically those transpiring at the spur of the moment. Finally, you learn how important it is to keep copies of your credit card and pay stubs. Keeping a copy of your stubs could be useful in the future, should you find any discrepancy in your credit report.

The main aim of this book was to educate you on the topic of credit repair and what you must do to fix yours. Regardless of whether you have a low score or a medium one, you can fix it just by taking a few steps in the right direction. One of the most important steps is to request your credit report from the credit bureaus or subscribe to a credit monitoring service, which will be sending you monthly credit reports from all the three main credit bureaus. Once you have done that, you must go through each credit report to check or ascertain the accuracy of all entries to ensure that they are correctly stated.

If anything is not stated, there could be other strategies we have discussed here that could work best for your situation. Simply follow that method to dispute any derogatory items from your credit report. As you do that, make sure not to give up too easily; the credit bureaus pry on people who give up on their rights. Even as you continue disputing derogatory items from your credit report, you need to study the relevant laws to ensure that you can use the law to your benefit even to get more derogatory items removed from your credit report.

Once your credit is repaired, you will feel happy and have a chance to buy a house, a car, secure your future, and more. You will also be able to make your family members happy and they will lead a merry life. You must save money. If you want to see your money grow, you have to make sacrifices. Find all the ways to make a living.

Many things can adversely affect your credit rating. Like late payments, multiple requests, billed accounts, judgments, mortgages, bankruptcies, and identity theft. Companies that sell credit repair secrets are likely to provide sample copies of the letters that can be sent to various credit bureaus and, possibly, to credit bureau addresses. This information is included in most credit repair kits. These credit repair secrets are available for free on the credit repair blog.

Whether or not you follow through with this dispute, there are many other methods you can and should use to maintain and increase your credit score. Always remember to watch your spending, pay your bills on time, and fight any errors that may be reflected in your credit score.

It is of utmost importance that you begin to put what you have learned to practice. Begin by requesting free credit reports and free credit scores from all the available bureaus. Any errors found in those credit reports should be immediately disputed so that you are no longer hurting your credit score with negative items. Following that, you should then be prepared to create a budget that will reinforce your new financial plan that is designed to increase your credit score. It is not too difficult, and you should be able to eliminate your unnecessary debts in the process.

Do not be afraid to live below your means if you must. It is a healthy tactic that can not only save money in the long run but may also expose you to a kind of life that is better suited to your tastes. Also, do not forget to overlook the obvious. If a late payment is leaving a black mark on your credit report then there is no reason to dismiss the idea of simply mailing a letter or making a phone call to explain what happened.

Remind them of your history with them and that your late payment was a one-time thing, and you'll find that your record may have the late payment removed.

This is perhaps one of the biggest lessons to take away from this book: be vigilant towards your credit report. There are many resources available and they are all viable. A bureau, a lender, a bank, and other financial institutions are all run by people, and people are prone to mistakes. It has been stated before, but it will be stated again for emphasis; do not let errors found on the credit go ignored. The damage they could cause should be eliminated as soon as possible. Lastly, be sure to tackle either the biggest debt first or the item that has the largest interest rate first. I hope you have learned something!

CREDIT SCORE SECRET:

A Complete Beginner's Guide On How To Repair Your Credit, Improve Your Score, And Boost Your Business. Including How To Write A 609 Dispute Letter.

Scott Moss

Table Of Contents

Introduction

Do you understand your credit score? You should. A credit score can decide your qualification for the nuts and bolts of life. Your credit rating influences your capacity to buy a home, land a decent financing cost on advances, or even find a new line of work. It speaks to the danger of non-installment that you present to a moneylender.

This book is written to provide information as accurate and reliable as possible. This book will learn all about what credit is and what you have to watch out for. You will find out how to spot negative items in your credit reports and learn about important strategies that you can employ to clean up your credit reports. Remember that you are not entirely helpless and hopeless if you have bad credit. You can repair your credit on your own.

After you have repaired your credit, you can use the tips in this book to keep your credit record clean at all times, learn about ways to rebuild your credit and work for financial freedom. These steps are not at all difficult to take. You simply have to be willing to take them.

We all want to have a nice credit rating because we understand that this makes access to credit easy and affordable; that's why we will do whatever it takes to ensure that we don't do anything that might threaten that rating. What happens when your efforts don't bear the needed result in boosting your credit rating? Credit repair might be the best solution for you. In any case, why should you pay more when you shouldn't? This book will walk you through the process of repairing your credit to ensure all negative items are removed from your credit report forever.

Nowadays, credit is extremely important given that most people use it almost every day, even without knowing, like it is a part of their daily survival. These include credit cards, house payments, and car payments, among others. Regrettably, many people fail to consider their credit rating until they run into trouble dealing with it.

When you have a bad credit rating, it can affect not only your ability to obtain a loan. It may also result in problems when securing any type of credit. For instance, you may encounter problems when renting a property, paying deposits on your phone lines, other utilities, or getting a store financing. As such, it is necessary to pay attention to your credit rating.

On the other hand, if you have a bad credit rating, there are several possible things that you can do to carry out a credit repair. The first crucial step is getting your credit report. You should know that all information regarding your credit is reported, by your bank and other financial institutions that you are involved with, to credit bureaus. In turn, the credit bureaus are the ones holding the key to start implementing the credit repair.

More often than not, people pay little attention to their credit reports unless they are already in a situation of credit repair. You must get a copy of your credit report regardless of what your credit rating reflects.

If you are attempting to carry out a credit repair, you need to look into your credit report. There are cases wherein credit reports have inaccuracies or discrepancies. For instance, your credit information may have been confused with another individual's file whom you have the same name with. There are also cases wherein there are erroneous data on your credit file. There are many cases in which people are surprised with reports of missing payments by mistake.

Should you find any inaccuracies or discrepancies in your credit report, you can carry out a credit repair by requesting, usually in writing, that the concerned credit bureau investigate the disputed items. In your request, you may include supporting documentation, if available, or simply state your dispute and request for an investigation.

If you're struggling with poor credit because of decisions on your part or something else, we will give you some tools to restore your good name and get you back on track. Most people struggle with a negative mark on their credit from time to time but don't be fooled into thinking there is no way back. Hopefully, by the time you finish reading this book, you'll be back on the road to a viable financial future with a more positive financial image to give to the world.

Here in this book is the answer you've been looking for. A chance to reclaim your life and provide you with everything you need to start again, on the right foot.

To reestablish a bad report, all you need do is to contract a specialist credit repair organization to do it for you or do-it-without anyone's help. The do-it-without anyone else's help strategy is good for individuals that want to dive deep into the procedures and understand how the system works.. In any case, you will probably still need a guide or manual to carry out the more technical aspects.

Good credit can help you out in life, and you can make a better score happen.

You need to have the best credit score if your goal is to easily and effortlessly secure an advance. You will likewise appreciate the perks that come with it as your credit rating goes up. One of the biggest advantages of having a superior credit score is having lower scheduled installments.

You can move in the direction of a noteworthy credit score by taking care of your tabs in time and guaranteeing that you utilize close to 30% of the credit you have accessible at a given time. You ought to likewise abstain from taking an advance except when you need it. Likewise, don't be enticed to utilize different credit extensions simultaneously. Moreover, check your credit reports in any event once in a year and check for any mistakes present.

CHAPTER 1:

Credit Score? What is it About?

WHAT IS CREDIT SCORE?

Credit score is the number derived after analyzing a person's financial records, particularly his credit history, to determine his creditworthiness level. It is a number that represents how well that person handles all the money that he borrows. It is the main determinant used by many lending companies, next to or together with the five C's of credit (character, capacity, capital, collateral, conditions). While the latter determines the creditworthiness of a person, the former objectively interprets it.

Most companies use numerous credit assessment measures to assess their potential borrowers' creditworthiness, but the credit score stands to be the most objective of all. Credit scores help many institutions in making financial and corporate decisions. Lending companies such as credit card companies, banks, and other financial institutions use the credit score to determine the possible risks they will face when lending money to a person.

They also use this score to evaluate the possible losses they might experience due to unpaid loans and bad debts. They also use this score to determine who are qualified to be their borrowers, the amount they will lend to them, the different terms and conditions that they may impose for each of them, and the interest rate they can charge to them.

For instance, obtaining credit is a person's option whenever he runs out of cash. He can still buy using a credit card issued by the lending company. However, issuing a credit card takes many steps, one of which is assessing his financial capability. The credit score will help lending companies in determining if he is a creditworthy person.

Creditworthiness is the measure of the possibility that a person will pay his financial obligations. Other countries, however, consider creditworthiness as the measure of the possibility that a person will fail to comply with his monetary obligations.

Creditworthiness is important in financial matters because lending companies also have to generate revenue from lending money. Suppose they do not check the creditworthiness of each of their borrowers. In that case, they may find themselves in bankruptcy either because their borrowers are cashless or because they already have left the country. Creditworthiness serves as a means to protect the interest not only of the lending company, but also of the public.

HOW CREDIT SCORES WORK

The key to improving your credit score is understanding what it is made of and how it works. If you can break it down into its components, you can tackle each one separately. It makes it simpler to understand what is coming from where, and how best and quickest to change things for the better.

HOW CREDIT SCORES ARE CREATED?

There are several different scoring systems available today. Each one has its proprietary algorithm and approaches things differently.

Each company or entity chooses which system to use. In a few cases, they may calculate your credit score using different methods before deciding.

FICO scores are by far the most used, with over 90% of credit institutions relying on them. Data analytics company FICO (formerly Fair Isaac Corporation) does not reveal its proprietary algorithm used to calculate the final score. But it is known that the formula relies on five major components, each weighted according to importance.

But, as already stated, FICO's is not the only current score calculation system out there. There are several others. Due to differences in the calculation mechanisms used, your score may differ by 100 points across different systems.

The FICO Scoring Model

FICO holds the most reliable scoring model thanks in no small part to its longstanding track record. Fair Isaac Company began computing these scores back in 1989. They have since revised the algorithms several times in the past over three decades to adjust for shifting factors to produce continuously dependable credit scores.

The ranges in between 600 and 740 mean from average to above average credit worthiness. In 2014, FICO introduced its FICO 9 scoring model.

The primary revision in this model was to reduce the importance of unpaid medical bills. The reasoning behind this is that medical debts that are not paid are not truly financial health indicators.

You might be waiting for insurance to pay a medical bill or simply be unaware that a medical bill had been given over to a collection agency. For some people, this critical change allowed their credit score to increase by up to 25 points.

Other changes in 2017 stopped collectors from reporting late medical debts that were not yet 180 days delinquent. Year 2017 also saw the three credit reporting bureaus drop all their data on civil judgments and the tax lien records from their files. FICO reported that this helped the scores of around six percent of consumers. Before FICO 9 came out, FICO 8 (that the company developed in 2009) was the standard credit score version. FICO 8 remains the most commonly utilized score of the lending industry. FICO 8's distinguishing features were to penalize you for charging near your total credit limit each month and provide pardon if you had only a single late payment of over 30 days.

It is worth noting that each time FICO releases an updated version on its scoring models, lenders may keep the version they are using or upgrade. FICO 8 has remained the overwhelming favorite because it costs so much to upgrade to the new model.

There are lenders still using even FICO 5 models. You can ask your lender which model they are using when you go through the application process.

FICO scores typically do not change that much over the short term. The exception is if you start missing payments or showing charge offs and defaults. Not everyone has a FICO score either. If you do not have credit, you will fall into the category of what experts call "credit invisible."

You must have six months of payments reported to the credit bureaus to have a FICO score.

Many people do not realize this, but it is a federal law that allows you to view your credit reports at least once a year. It might seem strange, but there was a time when you would not have been allowed to see what information had been collected about you. The credit bureaus felt that since you would not have been their primary consumer, they were not obligated to inform you about any information collected concerning you. However, a federal law issued about 25 years ago changed all of that. Now, you can check your report from each of these agencies at least once a year.

If you have not checked your report in a long time, it is strongly advised that you check all three. If you have checked it, it is recommended that you pull from one agency once every four months to see exactly what has changed on your report and make corrections as soon as they happen. Getting a copy is pretty easy. First, go to AnnualCreditReport.com and follow the instructions for requesting your report.

COMMONLY USED SCORING SYSTEMS

We have already mentioned the FICO score, which is the most widely accepted score calculation method. FICO uses several different scoring models, each designed for a specific purpose. Their NextGen scoring model, for example, is used to assess consumer credit risk, while the FICO SBSS is used to evaluate small businesses applying for credit.

FICO relies on the three national credit bureaus to calculate credit scores. These are Experian, Equifax, and TransUnion. Each of these credit bureaus may have different information on any one given consumer. In a bid to outcompete FICO, these same three bureaus collaborated to produce their credit scoring system. Known as the Vantage Score, it differs from FICO in several ways. A credit report created using the Vantage Score may show significantly different values than one for which FICO was used. Although not as commonly used as FICO, Vantage Score is also well-accepted by the financial community. Some financial institutions will pull credit reports from both systems for a consumer before deciding. There are some other scoring systems available too. CE Score is published by CE analytics. Currently, this score is made available to over 6,000 lending institutions across the U.S. And frequently, financial institutions may choose to use non-traditional credit scores to gain further insight into their consumers. Most of these scores are based on data not available to the national credit bureaus. Such credit scores may rely more on utility, rental, and telecom payment data. Public record information such as mortgages, property deeds, and tax records may also come into play.

CREDIT SCORE VALUES

Each time your credit score is calculated, it will come up with a specific value. The range for these values depends on the scoring system used. FICO and Vantage Score 4.0 (the latest Vantage Score model) calculate a score ranging from 300 – 850. Other scoring systems have entirely different scoring ranges. In general, though, one thing remains common across all orders: the higher your score, the better for you. While no calculation model is perfect, lending institutions still view consumers with a higher rating as carrying a lower risk. It makes them more likely to offer you their services and gets you a better deal.

As FICO is the most used credit score by far, we will take a closer look at how their credit ranges are broken down. The FICO Score 9 model is the most recent, but many institutions are still using the FICO 8 model so that we will break down below.

FICO SCORE 8 RANGES AND HOW LENDERS VIEW THEM

SCORE RANGE	CLASSIFICATION
300-559	Poor
560-669	Fair
670-739	Good
740-799	Very Good
800-850	Excellent

HOW CREDIT SCORES ARE CALCULATED

What your credit score reads is based on the factors considered when calculating it. These will vary significantly across different scoring systems, and even across different scoring models within the same network.

As mentioned previously, FICO and Vantage Score, while using different scoring algorithms, both rely on the data from the three national credit bureaus. That is Equifax, Experian, and TransUnion. Other, less traditional scoring systems may use only some of the information available from these three credit bureaus or none. They may choose to rely on data not available from these bureaus, such as rental and utility payment histories. Public record information, such as mortgages, liens, personal property titles, and deeds, is also frequently used. Each system will use a given set of data to calculate your credit score, assigning each component weight or importance. It usually comes through as each component contributing a specific percentage toward the final score. Some elements, such as your payment history, will weigh very heavily. Other things, like new credit, will have a much lower impact. Again, this varies according to the scoring system used.

CREDIT REPORT

The main document used by lending companies in computing a person's credit score is the credit report. It contains various personal and financial information of the individual such as the place they live, the specific manner through which they pay their bills, their current financial condition (whether they are currently bankrupt or insolvent), and whether they been sued for collection of money due to unpaid loans. Obtaining a credit report is free, so before a person applies for credit, they must get a copy of it. The Fair Credit Reporting Act (FCRA), the law governing the reporting of a person's credit information, requires every credit reporting company or agency to provide a person a free copy of their credit report once every year at their request.

WHAT'S A GOOD CREDIT SCORE?

In the current economy, it's a lot harder to qualify for a loan. Presently you need an excellent credit score to qualify for most types of credit. So what's a good credit score rating?

850 is immaculate credit and the most elevated credit score rating conceivable; however, I've never personally observed anybody with an 850. A good credit score begins in the 670 territory. Scores lower than 670 are not viewed as good credit.

In general, credit score values range from 300 to 850. A lower value means that a person is less creditworthy, while a higher value means that he is more creditworthy. However, this interpretation is broadened by the lending companies using their respective financial data on their clients. Instead of referring to a high or a low credit score, they have developed certain brackets that explain how creditworthy a person is. The following explains what each range of credit scores mean:

a. A credit score of 751 to 800 allows a borrower to apply for credit with the lowest interest rate and the most competitive amount because the lending companies have an assurance that he will not default in his monetary obligations. Many consider this score as the best. Someone who gets a score within this range can be almost certain their application will be granted.

b. A credit score of 711 to 750 allows a borrower to apply for credit at competitive interest rates. While the person's credit standing is relatively good, a slightly higher interest rate would be charged to them compared to someone who scores 751 and up. Someone who scores at this range gets a relatively good credit standing.

c. A credit score of 651 to 710 allows a borrower to apply for credit at moderate interest rates. This is the normal score that applicants must get to ensure that their application will be granted.

d. A credit score of 581-650 may be allowed to apply for credit, but he must obtain it at high interest rates. This is because at this range, the possibility of risks and loses is getting high.

e. A credit score of 300-580 does not allow a person to apply for credit. Their application may be granted, but they can only avail it if they are willing to pay the highest interest rate. This is because at this range, possibility of losses is very high.

However, one must take note that there is no general method in determining the credit score of a person. Its computation depends on the company assessing him. His credit score may be different when assessed by different companies, but also the range of scores may be interpreted to mean the same thing because of the elements considered in assessing him.

For instance, his score may be 375 in one company and 340 in another, but both scores mean that he is less creditworthy and has to repair his credit score fast.

HOW TO OBTAIN A GOOD CREDIT SCORE:

There are five criteria that your credit is scored upon which are rather simple to follow.

Your Payment History accounts for 35% of your credit score.

Do you pay your bills on time? If you don't do anything else yet make timely payments, you will have a good credit score in two years. Staying away from late payments is one of the most effective ways to support your credit. Otherwise your past actions will continue to harm your credit score. One ongoing multi day late payment will bring down your credit score, in all probability by 20! A few late payments and your score will drop extremely far, exceptionally fast. Being late by multiple days can hurt your score considerably more, and they are a main problem when assessing your credit score. Know that the later the wrongdoing, the more negative the impact on your score. While there is often a grace period, anything over 30 days will cause real damage to your credit score. Make sure to analyze your debt and check in with your bank statements. Be very diligent in making timely payments and deal with accounts before they are late or go to assortment. Try not to overextend yourself so that it harms your odds of making timely payments. If you have old late payments that can't be removed or fixed from your credit report, realize that time heals old injuries, and your score will increase if no new misconducts are reported. Always remember to pay before the "Grace Period" placed on your credit cards. Creditors charge extra expenses for late payments. This is an exceptionally enormous benefit for the banks. A bank may charge a $30-$35 expense for being 2 hours late on your payments! (be sure to look at the fine print on everything) Numerous banks have also introduced other feeds associated with multi-day late payments triggered even before the 30 days. Don't cut it too close with your due date. Get your payments in fast or set up automatic payments so you don't forget.

Amount Owed accounts for 30 Percent of your credit score.

The credit scoring model determines credit balance, usually against your high credit limit. This is calculated in rates. It's imperative to keep your balances as low as could be allowed. If you have a card with a $5,000 credit limit, keeping your balance beneath $500 places you in the 10% scope of accessible credit. There are thresholds in debt proportion that will make your credit score bounce higher. These thresholds are 70%, half, 30% and 10%. If you can't pay off your credit cards for the whole amount, pay them down BELOW the following conceivable edge. Calculate your credit limits along these lines. If you have a card with a $5,000 limit, increase 5000 x.10 (or.30,.50,.70) You will need to pay your balance for at least under these sums. For this situation - under $500 (or $1500, $2500 or $3500).

Keep in mind; the principal activity is to check your credit report for credit limits. If your high limit isn't reporting, the scoring model will utilize your balance as your credit limit. This implies you're utilizing 100% of your availability. Call your creditor and make sure they correct it. Conveyance of debt is a simple method to make sure you keep up a solid score.

Try to have a good spread of debt with a lower balance to limit proportion. For instance, it's better to have $2,000 debt on 5 cards than to have $10,000 on a card with all others paid off. In the case you're creeping up towards your credit limits, apply for more credit, or request an increase in credit from your current accounts.

This criterion depends on all out availability, not estimate of availability. It doesn't make a difference if you need $500 or $50,000. It's how you handle it that matters. Breaking debt onto extra cards or credit lines can assist you with raising your score rapidly.

The Length of Credit History counts for 15% of your credit score.

Length of credit history is about time the length or period you've had your credit accounts. If you've had a credit record open for 15 years, it is more stable than if you have had one for just two months. An important hint here is never to close your credit cards. Keep your old accounts open if they are in good standing, regardless of whether you don't utilize them and there's a zero balance. However, keep in mind that you need to use your credit lines a little to keep the active. Accounts unused for over 6 months become idle and are overlooked by the credit bureaus, except if there is a reprobate action joined to that record. Keeping your credit lines open likewise helps in improving your credit availability, clarified in the previous section. If you want to include credit, ask your card organization to increase your credit limit. The best way to increase your credit lines, beside getting another card, is to broaden your line on an old record with a good and long history. Be sure they report the credit amount increment to the bureaus accurately. A standard factor of amazingly good credit scores are long credit narratives. Credit reports that possess old accounts with a fifteen to twenty-year history will probably have a lot higher scores. In conclusion, it is important to add older stable credit lines to your report and keep them in good standing even when not using them.

Amount of New Credit accounts for 10 Percent of your credit score

New credit means fresh out of the box or newly opened accounts. If you have just opened your account you will need to build up its authority gradually. If you have recently applied for 10 credit cards, banks will, in general, accept the likelihood that possibly you've lost your employment and are needing a backup plan. Try to begin with one little credit extension and work from that point. Every time you start a new credit line, make sure that you can deal with the payments reliably, not be late, and keep your balances as low as is allowed, or paid off.

Kind of Credit Utilized accounts for 10% of your credit score.

The credit scoring model loves to see that you have an assortment of credit types in your file. The absolute best arrangement of credit is to have a home loan, a vehicle payment and a couple of credit cards. This credit is spread crosswise over various types of lenders and sort of credit reached out to you. There are a couple of types of credit to avoid. Payday loans are terrible to have credit with and your scores will likely be damaged for having these types of high-risk loans. Other very awful types of credit are the offers that enable you to have no payments for a year. These are hazardous, because the conditions of the understanding usually incorporate that if you don't pay the loan off in a year, on day 366 you will owe the whole years' worth of payments at normally 20% interest. This is a debacle already in the works. Individuals who more than once go for these offers are individuals who fall into credit difficulty. You ought not have that sort of credit on your credit report.

WHY USE DIFFERENT CREDIT SCORES INSTEAD OF JUST ONE?

This is a very important question with a very simple answer. There are many different credit scores out there, just like there are different cars such as pickup trucks and four-door sedans.

Imagine two cars that are about the same size and are nearly the same shape. They're hybrids that can be electrically charged or run on gasoline. They both have gears, steering wheels, comfortable seats, and four wheels. Yet, some people will go for one company's model while others will choose the other option.

People have different preferences when they select cars. It's a similar situation when it comes to credit scores. Some lenders prefer certain credit scores over the others. All credit bureaus use the information in your credit report. Still, their treatment of the information varies slightly as per certain lenders' needs, which is why there are different ranges and credit scores.

Therefore, it is important not to get too caught up in your credit score. The number has meaning for your lender and for that one transaction you'll be performing with them. The online credit scores are just a reference point for you to know how creditworthy your lender thinks you are. Taking this score to the lender, however, may not be enough to approve your loan.

They probably won't base their decision and subsequent loan on the online score you bring because they might just be using a different one than the one you brought. This may happen even if you bring the score from the same credit score developer.

A better idea would be to look at the range of the model used and see where you fall in that range. It would be in your interest to pay close attention to the risk factors statements that come with your score.

In case the lender is giving you the scores, it is a good idea to get the risk factor statements with those scores. If you have accessed the scores, you'll also get a list to see what has affected your scores the most and how they turned out.

You should tackle the issues mentioned in the risk factor statements first to be a less risky borrower. These statements will be very similar to each other regardless of the credit rating companies you used to get it. When you work on those issues, you'll be able to get better credit over time.

No one has a perfect credit score, ever, is that when you have credit you are carrying some risk, by definition. These risks will be shown in the credit scores you receive.

WHAT YOU NEED TO KNOW IF YOU HAVE NO CREDIT SCORE

Lack of information makes individuals have misbeliefs and misconceptions when it comes to issues relating to credit cards. You need to know some things to be well-informed about credit scores and what to do if you do not have a credit score.

It limits your options for credit score

For you to get credit, you need credit. Without a credit score, it makes it more difficult for you to get lenders that you can borrow from. Though it isn't impossible for you to get credit without your score, lenders need proof that you can make online payments, properly manage funds, *etc.* before they can decide to loan you. So, starting small with a student loan can help you make regular, on-time payments and build your score.

No credit score – bad credit

Not having a credit score might suggest that you've not needed a credit score, which isn't something bad. It also doesn't necessarily mean that you have a bad credit habit just as you might think.

Building a credit score takes time

To build your credit score, it means that you can repay an amount of debt over some time. This is no easy process which takes time since many factors contribute to your credit score. Once you have established a credit by obtaining a loan, you will begin to build your credit history and your credit score as soon as you pay back.

CHAPTER 2:

Get Your Credit Report

Finding your credit score online is easy but can also be dangerous. Hundreds of individual websites offer to check your credit quickly and usually for free, but the process itself requires you to provide extremely personal information to the sites. Sensitive personal information typically required includes your social security number, address, name, and sometimes a phone number. While these unofficial sites can potentially secure your credit score, they can sell your information and are generally not trusted.

Some of these sites are also related to identity theft. In general, you should never provide your full Social Security number online due to potential security risks. While there are dangers to finding your credit score online, there are ways to access the information securely. An essential factor to remember is that while most credit scoring sites these days offer free credit score checks, some will try to charge you. This is one red flag, and you should never pay for a credit check unless you have them all the time.

By law, you are allowed to check the top four lenders every year. Additionally, if your bill was declined on credit, you can view a denial report. The easiest way, but not the most convenient, is to contact every branch to check your credit: Experian, Equifax, TransUnion, and Innovis. A simple search allows you to find all the websites of the agencies mentioned. These agencies give you your credit score individually, but if you want a faster way to check your credit score, you can always use one of the objective credit checkers, which combine scores from three and sometimes four agencies. One of these sites is www.experian.com. Sites like Experian will also offer toll-free lines that you can use to check your credit score if you have any questions when providing information online.

However, be aware that all of the above agencies and websites will try to sell you packages and services designed to create, save, or protect your loan. While some of these services can be helpful, in general, spending and using credit responsibly is the best way to build or protect your credit score.

Knowing a person's credit rating has never been easier. Today, many online businesses are focused on providing credit reporting services. Anyone interested can search online to find the right service for their specific needs. It is true that in many ways, an individual's creditworthiness is like a brand. Many people and businesses will review this assessment and base their decision on whether or not to partner with an individual. However, what many people are not sufficiently aware of is that potential employers and colleges will also be looking through a prospective employee or student's records. A bad grade can lead a company or a school to decide not to do business with that person.

The downside of modern life is that a three-digit number can determine whether someone is considered worthy of association or not. That's why knowing your credit score is essential. With knowledge comes the ability to use that knowledge. If a person discovers that they have a low rating, they can actively improve themselves in several ways, such as debt consolidation or public debt grants and loans. In addition to a result considered "good", there are also ways to increase this number. In general, opening new credit accounts that an individual can quickly pay off over time will increase their credit score.

BE CAREFUL WITH FREE CREDIT SCORE WEBSITES

Hundreds of websites offer free credit scores. However, the truth is that many of these offers are not free. There are several different tips and methods by which you are tricked into parting with your hard-earned money.

The most popular websites offer a free credit report, but once you fill out many online forms, you are asked to pay a fee. Many will pay for it because they spent a lot of time filling out all the details and don't want to start repeatedly with finding another website or wasting more time.

There are other methods, when they do give access to your credit card information but then you are billed a month later for some service you didn't notice in the fine print and you have completely forgotten about it.

Now you know some things you need to pay attention to, but how can you find your credit score for free and avoid all the scam sites that seem to pop up everywhere?

While many companies and websites offer a free credit report, only a few can be trusted.

Search on Google and see how many sites there are. Look at reviews or ask around before giving your details. There are many ways to obtain credit score reports directly through the institutions, so you don't have to rely on sketchy websites.

Even when you have picked the right website, check the small print for extra services that might come up later.

HOW TO QUICKLY INCREASE YOUR CREDIT SCORE

There are many reasons why you may need to increase your credit score quickly. One of them is that some employers have recently started checking their potential employees' credit scores before hiring them. The reason is to ensure that employees can manage their finances and that their performance is not affected by financial difficulties. For people who are thinking of changing jobs but have lousy credit, now is the time to immediately consider taking steps to correct bad credit. Do not wait any longer.

Now the critical question is how to repair your bad credit effectively. Let me share with you some helpful steps:

Step 1: Find out your exact credit score.

Some like to assume that their credit scores are bad because they haven't made multiple payments before. This is wrong. You must know the exact credit score before you take any further action. If you want to be quick, you can check your credit score online at the AnnualCreditReport.com website. To play it safe, you should also get a credit report from one of the major credit bureaus, i.e., Experian, TransUnion, or Equifax. Once you know your credit score, you need to plan the appropriate strategies to improve it. We remind you to carefully review your credit report to make sure there are no errors. If you notice an incorrect report, you should contact your credit bureau to correct the mistake immediately.

Step 2: Collect money to pay off your past debts

No matter how bad your credit report is, it would help if you always faced it with courage. If you have past debts that you have not yet paid off, it is advisable to raise funds to pay off the debts. Don't be afraid to connect with collection agencies. Obtain their consent to remove negative entries from your report after paying your debts. If you can't pay off the debt all at once, you can negotiate with them to pay it off in installments. Never run away from debt collection agencies as this will worsen your credit rating.

Step 3: Budget to pay your monthly bills

In addition to managing your old debts, you should also keep an eye on your checking accounts. You must make your monthly payments on time. This way, you can gradually increase your credit rating.

For example, if you have a credit card in hand, you will be reminded to make sure there is no unpaid balance on your monthly statement.

The truth is that no matter how bad your credit score may seem now, there are ways and strategies to fix it. It all starts with budgeting and paying off debt.

Slowly and with the right information you will get a better handle on the situation and handle your finances with ease.

If you cannot deal with lenders to increase your credit score, it is best to seek a professional counselor who continually deals with these issues.

After a few steps, it will help you improve your credit score.

MORE TIPS ON HOW TO INCREASE YOUR CREDIT SCORE

Achieving and maintaining a high credit rating is not that difficult. At least when you know what it does, it will become straightforward and you will wonder why you struggled with this for so long in the past. You need to do many things to get a high score, and there are some things you need to do to increase your score.

Let's see what you can start doing right now to make the most significant difference.

Tip 1 - Too Much Credit is Bad!

If you've made the mistake of opening too many credit cards and too much line of credit, you may be keeping your score low without even realizing it. Having a lot of credit available is excellent, but you never want to stretch yourself too far and negatively affect yourself. Not more than 3 to 5 revolving accounts (credit card accounts) must be opened simultaneously. You will also want to save the balance on low cards, the higher the balance, the less credit you have available which will bring the score down!

Tip 2 - Be careful with whom you have the opportunity to settle your loan!

A few years ago, I made this mistake when I authorized several car dealerships to handle my loans, and they also applied for sales cards within a few weeks. My rating was around 720, and it dropped to 680 just for all the apps I had. Every time my credit was taken, it fell like a rock! Whatever the reason, credit bureaus don't like your loan to be spent in a short period.

Tip 3 - Check Your Credit Report for Common Mistakes!

Most credit reports will contain some errors. Just go through the report and find anything that doesn't look right or is a separate error.

You will have the option to dispute the records and delete them. This will quickly increase your credit score! Many people don't realize that mistakes are always there, but few people "make mistakes". Take a look at yours, or you might miss it!

THE SIMPLE STEPS TO IMPROVING YOUR CREDIT VALUE

1. Always pay your bills on time!

2. Live below your means!

3. Save money in your savings account for small and large purchases. If you don't need it, please don't buy it! If you want it, save it!

4. Every six months, check your credit reports for errors, inaccuracies, incorrect data, duplicates, and negative loans that are outdated. A FREE loan report can be obtained once a year online at annualcreditreport.com. If you want to check your credit reports more than once a year, you can buy them for around $9 from each credit bureau. If you get your credit reports in your annual account or at one of the credit bureaus, the results will not go down.

5. Keep your credit card balance low by about 1/3 of the limit. Never exceed this amount and never increase your credit card; it will lead to lower credit scores.

Be aware that some credit card companies reduce consumption limits for no reason and without notice above maximum credit limits.

6. Open two or three revolving credit cards at the same time. Having too many revolving credit cards open, even if your balance is zero, shows that you could go out tomorrow and increase your credit card limits. If you are closing accounts, you will want to close new ones, NOT old ones. Older people give you a higher credit score. Loan companies respect the opening period for credit card accounts. They usually require at least a year or two of on-time payment.

7. If you have your driver's license number on your driver's license, replace it with your usual computer-generated name. If you lose your driver's license, you have all the information someone needs to remove your credit identity. They can use your data to get credit, buy things online, get credit cards, etc.

If your Social Security number is deducted from your driver's license, it will also prevent auto repair shops from running credit reports without your approval. Some agents will ask you to provide a driver's license for insurance purposes. Still, they use your social security number, name, and address to write up a credit report on you and see if you have enough credit before spending more time with you.

8. Unsubscribe from pre-approved spam by calling: 1-888-303-7722

9. Don't accidentally apply for a loan or add your social security number in forms. Loan applications appear as inquiries on your credit report, signaling lenders that you may be taking on new debt. Tip: Insurance companies now ask for your social security number to make you an offer. Don't apply for a loan often (this is called a hard move); your goal here is to keep your credit reports from showing excessive demands that will hurt your credit score.

10. Lenders want to see stability. It means living in the same place for more than two years, staying in the same job/career for more than two years, etc. If you are moving often, get a mailbox to make it look more stable.

11. If you have billing accounts, agree to a lower amount (called your debt settlement). This will save you money, but keep in mind that it doesn't mean the item will be deleted from your credit report. A "paid collection" will be displayed, but it's better than an "open collection". You may perform credit repairs to remove derogatory items from your credit reports when they are paid or not. Government law, the Fair Credit Reporting Act, states in Section 611 that if an item on a credit report is inaccurate, out of date, duplicated, misleading, or cannot be verified, it must be removed or corrected.

The law says the consumer has the right to an accurate credit report. The statistics are staggering, given the number of mistakes the agency makes regarding people's credit reports.

12. Also, if collection agencies call you, you should exercise your right under the Fair Debt Collection Practices Act and ask them to "verify the debt". This will accomplish four things: 1. show that this unknown company has the right to collect the alleged debt; 2. that an unnamed company proves that the debt is valid; 3. prevent them from making annoying phone calls, and 4. prevent them from adding another negative tag to your credit report.

13. Any change in your credit report can dramatically affect your results. For example, merely closing two accounts not only reduces the number of accounts opened in slices (which will usually improve your score) but also reduce the total number of all open accounts (which generally reduce the score). Likewise, such action will affect all accounts' average age, which could increase or decrease the count. As you can see, one simple change affects a lot of items on your credit report. Therefore, it is impossible to give a 100% estimate how a particular action will affect your credit score.

CHAPTER 3:

The FICO Scoring Model

Most people do not realize that the credit bureau that issues your reports does not determine your score, another company does it, a third party called the Fair, Isaac Corporation (FICO). They weigh all the different elements of your credit report to determine what number you get. All the data collected by the credit bureaus are factored in to come up with a three-digit number.

This is probably the only grade you should seriously worry about after you get out of school. It is the grade you get for your financial stability. That single three-digit number will tell the world what they should think about you. But it is not a number that reflects only the present it is also a pathway to your future. If anything is wrong with your reports, it is your responsibility to get it fixed. This is the primary and most effective way to change it.

Thus, you must know what's in your report so that you can correct any incorrect or incomplete information. This will help to bring your score up higher. Very few people have a perfect score, but you can improve that number if you know what to do.

UNDERSTANDING FICO CREDIT SCORE

FICO Scores are numerous elements almost all lenders in the U.S. think about when they settle on key credit choices. A US News and World Report article expressed that "The FICO Score is the No. 1 bit of information to decide the amount you'll pay on a loan and whether you'll get credit." Such choices incorporate whether to endorse your credit application, what credit terms to offer you, and whether to expand your credit limit once your credit account is built up. FICO Scores are utilized by many creditors, including the 50 biggest lenders, making it the most generally utilized credit score. At the point when you acknowledge new credit and oversee it tenaciously by reliably paying as agreed, you show to lenders that you don't have credit hazard. Lenders utilize your credit history as a method for assessing how well you have dealt with your credit till date.

A FICO Score is a three-digit number determined from the credit information on your credit report at a customer reporting agency (CRA) at a specific point in time. It outlines your credit report's information into a solitary number that lenders can use to survey your credit chance rapidly, reliably, unbiasedly, and fairly.

Lenders will utilize your FICO Scores to assess your credit hazard—and proceed with your application. It is also an objective measure that you obtain depending on your genuine acquiring and repayment history without being influenced by other types of information, for example, race or religion.

Your FICO Scores from every agency might be diverse because FICO Scores depend exclusively on the particular credit information in that agency's credit file. Not all lenders report to each of the three CRAs. Indeed, even in situations where the lender reports to each of the three CRAs, the result may appear different depending on the evaluation process.

Notwithstanding the three-digit number, a FICO Score incorporates "score factors" which are the top factors that make up your score. Tending to these score variables can assist you with improving your monetary wellbeing after some time. Having a good FICO Score can place you in a superior situation to qualify for credit or better terms later on.

Lenders use FICO Scores regarding a wide assortment of credit Items such as:

• Credit Cards

• Auto Loans

• Personal Loans & Lines of Credit

• Student Loans

• Home Equity Lines & Loans

• Mortgages

FICO or the Fair Isaac Company, in particular, calculates your credit score based on 5 things:

Payment History: 35%

Length of your Credit History: 15%

Type of Credit Utilized: 10%

New Credit Taken On: 10%

Amount Owed to Lenders in Total: 30%

What do these values mean? It means that some things will have a larger effect on your credit score. If you miss any payments or don't make them on time, that will change your credit score more than, say the total amount of debt you have (amount owed to lenders in total). Both of these factors have a high significance and should be taken very seriously. Another thing that is covered in the amount that you owe is your utilization. This shows the amount of debt you have taken on as compared to your available limit on credit. If 30% or more of your credit limit is utilized, it will likely negatively affect your score.

720 and Above Excellent

When you have this score, you get the best interest rates and repayment terms for all loans. This score can come in handy if you are hoping to make some major purchases. You will be able to get credit without any problems and at the lowest possible rates. But then, this score is extremely hard to establish. You will have to put in a lot of effort to maintain this score and still, you will not come anywhere close to 800. The most you can wish to come close to is 720 and remain there for as long as possible.

680-719-Good

When you are in this category, you will get good rates and terms but not as good as those with excellent scores. With this score, you can get favorable mortgage terms. You might not face as many problems but will have to be ready to run around from company to company to approve your credit. Again, this score is not very common. You need to put in extra effort to get it over the 680 mark.

If you cannot cross this limit because of some erroneous charges, you must try your best to get it cleared as soon as possible.

620-679-Average

When you are in this category, you can get fair mortgage terms and have it easy when buying smaller ticket items, (of course with no better rate than good and excellent scores). Take care not to slip down to the level where a mortgage plan is unaffordable.

580-619-Poor

When you are at this level, you only get credit on the lenders' terms. You will probably pay more to access credit so be ready for extra charges. You should also remember that you cannot access auto financing if your score goes lower than this range so you should work towards building it. This is where a large majority of individuals lie. Their score will be bad mostly owing to wrong entries. If you are here, then you will have a tough time getting credit within your budget limits and will have to be ready to pay up a lot of money.

500-579-Bad

If your credit score is in this range, access to credit will cost you dearly. If you are looking for a 30-year mortgage, you could be looking at 3% higher interest rates than how much you would pay if you had good credit. On the other hand, if you are looking for something short time like a 36-month auto loan, you will probably pay almost double the interest rate you would pay if you had good credit. So being here is probably the worst thing that can happen to your credit report. It is almost impossible to get low interest rates.

Less than 500

If your credit score goes to this level, it is so bad that it might be almost impossible to get any type of financing. If you do, the interest rate will simply be unfathomable. You might have to spend 30 to 40 years trying to repay it. Your entire life will be dedicated toward repaying a loan that is not worth it.

I am sure several of you are in this last range. But do not panic as help is at hand. You might wonder if it is possible for you to fix your score if you are in this category and the answer is yes! You can improve your credit score and possibly enter the good range.

WHAT ABOUT THE OTHER THREE FACTORS? WHAT DO THEY MEASURE?

Firstly, the longer the time you have credit, the better you will be in the lender's eyes. This determines the length of your credit history.

Think of this as relevant experience on your credit value; the more you have, the higher your credit score will be. A reasonable and sizeable 15% of your credit score has been attached to your report for this reason.

Secondly, if you've applied for credit recently, it accounts for 10% of your score. Think of this as recent relevant experience— except instead of getting a good job, you get good credit. The last thing that the credit companies look for to determine your credit score is the different credit types you have. An example of this is that a person is likely to have slightly better credit than you if they have a car loan and a mortgage on their credit report along with credit cards, while yours only has credit card accounts.

HOW FICO SCORES HELP YOU

A FICO Score gives lenders a quick, objective and predictable gauge of your credit risk. Before using scoring, the credit allowing procedure could be moderate, conflicting, and unjustifiably one-sided. Here are a few different ways FICO Scores help you.

Get credit quicker

FICO Scores can be conveyed immediately, helping lenders accelerate credit card and loan endorsements. This implies when you apply for credit, you'll find a solution immediately, even within seconds. Indeed, even a home loan application can be endorsed a lot quicker for borrowers who score over the lender's base score necessity. FICO Scores likewise permit retail locations, web locales, and different lenders to make "moment credit" decisions. Remember that FICO Scores are just one of numerous factors lenders think about when settling on a credit decision.

Credit decisions are more attractive

Utilizing FICO Scores, lenders can concentrate on the realities identified with credit risk, instead of their genuine beliefs or inclinations. For example, factors such as sexual orientation, race, religion, nationality, and conjugal status are not considered by FICO Scores. So when a lender utilizes your FICO Score, it is assessing your credit history that is reasonable and objective.

A Higher FICO Score sets aside you cash

When you apply for credit – regardless of whether it's a credit card, a vehicle loan, an individual loan or home loan – lenders need to see how risky you are as a borrower to settle on an appropriate number. Your FICO Scores may influence not just a lender's decision to give you credit, but also how much and what rate.

Think about these two models:

Two individuals are getting $230,000 on a 30-year contract. A borrower with FICO Score of 760 could pay $211 less every month in interest in contrast to a borrower with a FICO Score of 630. That is an investment funds of $75,960 over the life of the loan.

On a $20,000, 48-month automobile loan, the borrower with a FICO Score of 720 could pay $131 less every month in interest compared to a borrower with a FICO Score of 580. That is a total of $6,288 over the life of the loan.

Many people do not realize this, but it is a federal law that allows you to view your credit reports at least once a year. It might seem strange, but there was a time when you would not have been allowed to see what information had been collected about you. The credit bureaus felt that since you would not have been their primary consumer, they were not obligated to inform you about any information collected concerning you. However, a federal law issued about 25 years ago changed all of that. Now, you can check your report from each of these agencies at least once a year.

If you have not checked your report in a long time, it is strongly advised that you check all three. If you have checked it, it is recommended that you pull from one agency once every four months to see exactly what has changed on your report and make corrections as soon as they happen. Getting a copy is pretty easy. First, go to AnnualCreditReport.com and follow the instructions for requesting your report.

CHAPTER 4:

The Difference Between FICO and Other Credit Scores

DIFFERENT BUREAUS USE DIFFERENT MODELS FOR CREDIT SCORE CALCULATION

There are different scores that lenders can get from the different bureaus and the score for one may not mean the same thing as the other. This is important because when you get your credit score, it is imperative that you know exactly what your number means and if you're in hot water or not. There are different credit scoring ranges for different lenders. Here are the most popular ones:

a) FICO Credit Scoring Range

Extension of Range: 350-850 is the credit score range. The Fair Isaac Corporation's credit score is what many lenders see when they look at your credit report.

This score is one of the most used out there. The FICO score shows how creditworthy you are in the eyes of lenders.

There's not just one type of FICO score as new next generation/NextGen scores have been introduced that go up to 950.

b) Vantage Score Credit Scoring Range

Extension of Range: 501-990. The Vantage Score credit scoring model is formed by the 3 major credit bureaus, namely TransUnion, Equifax and Experian.

When you receive your credit score from one of these bureaus directly, they will most likely give you this Vantage Score. It is also referred to as the Vantage Score 2.0 model.

c) Vantage Scores 3.0 Credit Scoring Range

Extension of Range: 300-850. This credit scoring model is largely similar to the previous one (Vantage Score 2.0 Model). The only big difference is that the range is slightly larger for the Vantage Score 3.0 Range, i.e. 300-850.

d) Trans Risk Credit Scoring Range

Extension of Range: 300-850. This range is used by the credit bureau Trans Union when they are trying to pin your creditworthiness down.

e) Equifax Credit Scoring Range

Extension of Range: 280-850. This is the scoring range used by the credit bureau Equifax, to show how risky it is to lend to you.

f) Experian Plus Credit Scoring Range

Extension of Range: 330-830. This one is used by the credit bureau Experian and is how that credit bureau shows how creditworthy you are.

THE DIFFERENCE BETWEEN FICO AND OTHER CREDIT SCORES

Another question that you may have along the way is the differences between the FICO score and the other credit scores. To get started, these scores are the only ones created by the Fair Isaac Corporation, and they are used by about 90 percent of the top lenders when it is time to make lending decisions overall.

The reason for this is that FICO scores will be seen as the standard when it comes to making fair and accurate decisions about an individual's creditworthiness.

Now there are other credit scores out there, and they can be used in some situations. These other scores will calculate the number they give you differently than the FICO score can. So, while it may seem like some of those other scores are similar to what we see with the FICO score, they aren't. Only FICO scores will be used by most of the top lenders you want to borrow from, and while the others can be good for some monitoring of your score, if you would like, the best way to go is with the FICO score.

CHAPTER 5:

Why is it so Important to Have a Good Credit Score?

When you apply for credit, insurance, telephone service and even a place to live, providers want to know if you have a good risk level. And to make that decision, they use credit scores.

A credit score is a number. A high score means you have good credit. A low score means you have bad credit.

A higher score means that you represent a lower risk and are more likely to get the product or service - or pay less.

It works as follows: Credit managers extract information from your credit reports, such as your bill payment history, your accounts' age, your unpaid debts and the collection actions initiated against you.

Credit scores can be used in various ways. These are some examples.

1.**Insurance companies** use the information in your credit report and combine it with other factors to predict the probability that you present an insurance claim and predict the amount you could claim. They consider this information to decide if they will grant you insurance and how much they will charge you.

2.**Public service companies** use credit scores to decide if they will require a new customer deposit to provide the service. Cell phone providers and homeowners who rent homes also use scores when considering a new client or tenant.

Each type of company has different scoring systems, and credit scoring models can also be based on other information apart from your credit report's data. For example, when you apply for a mortgage loan, the system can consider the amount of the advance, the total amount of your debts and your income.

ACCESS TO BEST CREDIT CARDS

Having a good credit score is an essential factor to qualify for an opportunity to get a credit card that provides excellent cash-back reward programs, awesome advantages, low rates and so many others. Besides paying lower interest and fees, having access to the best credit card means you can get a larger credit limit. Therefore, you can have freedom and flexibility to make purchases you want without the financial constraint that arises from a small credit limit.

An increase in your credit limit results into an increase in your creditworthiness overtime. This shows banks and other lending institutions that you are mature enough and can handle the responsibility of having access to a large amount of credit.

Having a good credit score can help you discover cards with cash-back rates as high as 5% at different places like restaurants, grocery stores, E-commerce platforms, gas stations and any other time your card is used.

EASY ACCESS TO LOAN

Having a bad credit history will make you scared of applying for a new credit card or loan due to the fear of being turned down. Maintaining a good credit score tells a lot about your credit responsibility. When banks and lending institution see your credit score, they can be rest assured that they are not at risk and you are likely to pay back the money you are asking them to loan to you. Though this does not guarantee an outright approval because other factors such as your income, debts, etc. are also considered, it just provides you with a very good chance of getting approval.

LOWER INTEREST RATES ON LOANS

The interest rate that you get to pay is directly dependent on your credit score. Suppose you have a very good credit score. In that case, you might not need to consider the interest rate when applying for a credit card because you will always qualify for the best interest rates thereby paying very minimal charges on credit card loans. If you always want your interest rate to be low, you need to have a good credit score.

EASY APPROVAL FOR RENTAL OF HOUSES AND APARTMENT

So many landlords and apartment owners tend to check credit scores for the same reason lenders do routinely. They fear that tenants with bad credit score might be unable to keep up with rent payment and avoid the hassle – they avoid tenants with a high risk. Having previous bad credit scores gives the property owner an unsettled mind that you might not be able to pay back at the stipulated time, a good credit score says otherwise.

BETTER JOB APPLICATIONS

This is not the only criteria considered by employers, however, so many employers access the credit history of various job seekers during their application processes especially when the job you're applying for requires handling money or accessing clients' sensitive financial information. Majority of employers believe that your ability to use credit responsibly makes you more likely to be a responsible employee.

NEGOTIATING POWER

You can get leverage to negotiate a lower interest rate on your student loan, new credit card, mortgage and others if you have a good credit score. Having a credit card with a history that doesn't have an iota of problems provides you with more bargaining power, that is needed to secure the favorable terms that you need. You therefore can carefully pick the terms that will be of great advantage to your present financial circumstance.

CHAPTER 6:

What Affects My Score?

PAYING LATE OR NOT AT ALL

One of the worst things that you can do when it comes to your credit score is paying late on anything. About 35 percent of your score will be about your history of making payments so if you are not on time this will cause a huge drop. Consistently being late on these payments is going to cause a lot of damage to your credit score. Always pay your bills on time, especially your credit card bills.

What is even worse than paying late is not paying at all. If you decide to completely ignore your cards and other bills and not pay them at all, then you are going to be in even more trouble as well. Each month that you miss out on a payment for your credit card, you will end up with one month closer to helping your account be charged off.

If you ever want a chance to get your credit score up at all, especially if you are hoping to get it up to 800 or higher, then you have to stop the late payments. This will be a bad thing because it shows that you are not willing to pay your money back, and they are less likely to give you more money in the process.

For those struggling with making payments, whether these payments are often late, or they don't come in at all, it is time to get a budget in place. You live above your means, which is never a good sign of getting your score up to where you would like. When you can get your budget in place and start paying your debts on time, you will be able to get that credit score higher in no time.

HAVING AN ACCOUNT CHARGED OFF OR SENT TO COLLECTIONS

Next on the list is having your accounts charged off. When creditors are worried that you will never pay your bills for loans or credit cards, they will use a process known as charging off your accounts. A charge off means that the insurer has pretty much given up on ever hearing from you again. This does not mean that you are no longer going to hold responsibility for this debt at all. This is one of the absolute worst things out there when it comes to your credit score.

Another issue is when one of your accounts is sent off for collections. Creditors often work with debt collectors to be able to collect their payments. Collectors could send your account to collections after, but sometimes before, charging it all off. This is never a good thing, even if the account is charged off at that time, either. If you are at the point of your bills going to collections or being charged off, this means that you have not just missed one or two payments. It means that you have gone so long without paying the whole thing that the company figures they will never get it back. Either they have probably written it off as a tax break or they have sold it to a credit collection company that will be bothering you a lot in the future.

This is never a good thing. You are going to be harassed for a long time to pay back your debt. It will show other creditors that you have not just missed a few payments when things get tough. It shows them that you fell so far behind that someone else, someone who had given you money in the past, decided to give up on you in the process. This is hard to fight against and will not make a new creditor feel like they should loan you the needed money.

FILING BANKRUPTCY

This is a bit extreme that you should try to avoid at all costs. Bankruptcy is an extreme measure, and it will cause a lot of devastation to the score that you are working with. It is also going to be on your record for seven to ten years. It is a good idea to discuss all your alternatives with an advisor before filing for bankruptcy.

You need to do everything you can to avoid bankruptcy at all costs. It may seem like the best idea to work with. You assume that you can just walk away from all of the debt that you have and not have to worry about it ever again when you declare bankruptcy. This is not really how this whole process is going to work for you at all, though.

There are several types of bankruptcies that you can work with, but you will often need to go through and pay off as much of the debt as possible. And sometimes, this can be several years of making payments and having your wages confiscated and taken away before you can even get to the bankruptcy. You could just pay the debts for that amount of time instead or make some kind of agreement with the creditors for a lower amount if needed, and now have the black mark of the bankruptcy on your side.

Once the bankruptcy is complete, which can take some time, then a new problem will occur. You have to then focus on how you will handle the black mark on your credit report for quite a bit of time. This could be anywhere from seven to ten years. And you can bet that creditors are not going to look kindly on all that stuff. You will find that it is almost impossible to get any kind of credit or any other monetary help you need for a long time afterward. To avoid bankruptcy, you need to learn how to work with a budget and figure out the best ways to manage your money, no matter what the income is that you are working with. This is easier to manage than you may think and can help you get on a good payment schedule to deal with your debts and get them paid off. The bankruptcy seems like an easy way to get out of the debt. Still, it haunts you for many years afterward. It can make getting credit later on almost impossible, and it will not solve the underlying problem that got you into this situation.

CLOSING AN OLD CREDIT ACCOUNT

It has been observed that closure of old credit accounts leads to a drop on the credit score, most especially if the card has a balance. The age of your credit history is typically one of the factors used to calculate your credit scores.

There's always an average age of all your credit accounts, closing an old account will cause the average age of your account to drop thereby reducing the overall credit age you have available on your credit accounts. This pushes down your credit usage and could hurt your score.

MAKING A NEW APPLICATION FOR LOAN OR CREDIT

Anytime you apply to get a loan, the financial institution will most-likely carry out a "credit application search" on your report, which has to be authorized by you before making a decision is made either to end lend you not.

This credit application search could reduce your credit score by an insignificant amount. The harm it can do to your account becomes enormous when you repeatedly make requests within a short timeframe.

You should ensure that you are in dire need of funds before applying for credit, to avoid drops on your credit score from constant checks.

DEROGATORY FINANCIAL SETTLEMENTS

Declaring yourself legally bankrupt has grave implications on your credit score and can significantly harm your score. There are some other derogatory financial settlements such as tax evasions, and civil judgements, among others, that could be of harm to your credit score.

These items show that you cannot take care of your funds properly, and you are a risky individual to lend money to.

HIGH BALANCES OR MAXED OUT CARDS

You always need to take a look at the balances that you will have on your credit cards all of the time. The second most important part that comes with our credit score is the amount of debt on them, which will be measured by credit utilization. Having high balances for credit cards, relative to the credit limit you are working with, will increase credit utilization and make your credit score go down. For example, if you have a limit of $10,000 on a card, but the balance is at $9500 or higher, your score will not positively reflect this one.

You also need to make sure that you are not maxing out or going over the limit regarding our credit cards. Credit cards that are over the limit or maxed out will make the credit utilization that you have at 100 percent. This will be one of the most damaging things that you can do with your credit score. Make sure to paydown those debts as fast as possible to maintain your credit score and keep it from plummeting.

CLOSING CREDIT CARDS

There are a few ways that closing your card will end up with a decrease in your credit score. First, you need to take a look at closing a card that still balances it. When you close that card, the credit limit you get to work with will end up at $0, while your balance is still going to be the same. This will make it look like you have maxed out the credit card, which will cause your score to drop a bit. If you want to close your account, you need to make sure that you pay off the balance before closing it.

Another thing to consider is what will happen when you close your old credit cards. About 15 percent of your credit score will be the length of your credit history, and longer credit histories will be better. Closing old cards, especially some of the oldest cards, will make your history seem like it is a lot shorter than it is. Even if you do not use the card anymore, and there are no annual fees, you should keep the card open because you are losing nothing and gaining more.

And finally, we need to be careful about closing cards that have available credit. If you have more than one credit card to work with, some that have balanced and some without, then closing the cards that do not have a balance will increase the credit utilization. You can just keep those all out of the way and see your credit report go up.

NOT HAVING ENOUGH MIX ON THE REPORT

While this is not as big of a deal as some of the other options, you will find that having a good mix of credit will be about 10 percent of your credit score at the time. If you have a report that only has one or two things on it, such as either credit cards or loans, it is likely the score you are working with will be affected somehow.

The more you can mix up your accounts and get them to have many different things on them, the better. You don't want to overextend yourself, but having a mix of loans, mortgage, credit cards, and more, that you pay off each month without fail, is going to be one of the best ways that you can raise your credit score without causing harm or paying too much in the process.

This does not mean that you should go out and apply for many different things all at once to get your mix up. This is something that often happens; naturally, the longer you work on your credit score. You may have a few credit cards, and then you take out a loan for a car and pay it off. Maybe you need a loan for a vacation or some home improvement, so you will have those accounts and then get a mortgage.

As time goes on, these different loans and credit amounts will come and go, but they will all show up in the credit mix and help increase your score. If you try and increase your mix all at once, you will bring up some red flags against your credit, which can cause issues as well. Doing this over a few years is the best way to make sure that your credit score goes up.

APPLYING FOR TOO MUCH

Another thing that is going to count on your report is the credit inquiries. These will take up about 10 percent of the score that you work with. Making several applications for loans and credit in a short amount of time will cause a big drop in your credit score along the way. Always keep the applications for credit to a minimum, so this doesn't harm you along the way.

In some cases, this is not going to harm you too much. For example, if you have a good credit score and you want to apply for a mortgage, you will want to apply for a few mortgages and shop around a bit. If you do these close together, it will not be seen as bad because the lender will assume this is what you are doing, rather than you taking on too much or that you have been turned down. You can also explain this to them easily if they ask. For most other cases, though, this is not going to be a good sign. Having all of those inquiries on your score will slightly lower it, at least for the short term. And when other lenders see that you are applying for a lot of credit, they will assume that you are getting rejected. They will wonder why or they will assume that you are taking on too much credit that you will not handle, and they will not want to lend you any money either. These are just a few of the different things that you are going to work with when the time comes to handle your credit report. Sometimes the things that can harm your score are going to be much more important than the things that can help improve the score. Working on both is going to be important when it all comes down to it as well, and knowing how to avoid some of the common things that can ruin your credit in no time is imperative to getting that score up and seeing it work the way that you want.

CHAPTER 7:

Commitment, Discipline and the Right Mindset will Make the Difference!

AVOIDING THE BAD CREDIT WITH THE RIGHT MINDSET

A perspective towards money is an overarching mentality you have about your finances. It influences the way you make important financial choices every day.

It will significantly affect your potential to attain your goals. If you shift your perspective on income, you continue to make smarter choices on how problems can be solved.

The influence of constructive thought does indeed apply in this situation.

FEATURES OF A BAD MONEY MINDSET

Your attitude towards money is like moral fatigue-it pushes you to act.

If you have a positive mentality about finances, you are more likely to be confident and take the measures you need to take to be effective.

On the other hand, negativity is generating emotions which prevent action:

- Fear or intimidation

- Defeatism

- Procrastination

It's harder to see the way ahead as you shift your attitude towards money and concentrate on the benefits of what you should achieve.

A fresh outlook on money will help you easily reach your goals. So how do you build a positive mentality around money?

QUALITIES OF A POSITIVE MONEY MINDSET

Once you accept financial positivity, you begin to understand that no issue is impossible. This will be done whether you have $5,000 in interest, or $50,000. Your credit score may be 500 but no loan limit would last forever.

When you have a good attitude about your finances, you start searching for possibilities instead of seeing roadblocks and realize that any financial problem is fixable.

The secret to success is to resolve negative feelings, to concentrate on the optimistic.

EMPLOYING A POSITIVE MONEY MINDSET TO CIRCUMVENT FINANCIAL CHALLENGES

Positivity may be tough to cultivate while you are in a stressful position, but it is important.

Let's assume you have those above $50,000 credit card debt issue. There are probably several factors which drive your negativity:

• The total monthly contributions are about $1,250 and the budget is close

• But despite spending too much, the balances never seem to drop

• High interest rates currently make up approximately 60% of every investment you make

• Therefore, if you adhere to the minimal contributions it would take more than 40 years to recover everything you owe.

The first step to paying off debt and changing your financial behaviors is to adjust the way you think about income. By reflecting on what debt-free life would feel like, gaining financial security, and getting the freedom to invest your money on the stuff you enjoy most, remaining focused and meeting your financial objectives is much simpler.

Your strategic emphasis needs to be on seeking alternatives. You 're not the first one to slip into debt so fast. Start from what you know: Minimal payments will not create an impact sufficiently, so you need a better plan. If you just repay the bills at $1,250 instead of meeting the full payment plan the condition changes significantly. It will only take 62 months, instead of 502 months to meet the payout deadline. In reality, five years is a fair amount of time needed for a debt repayment strategy.

FIND FINANCIAL BALANCE

Attitude is not the only component of a positive financial mindset. You need harmony too. Stability is what fosters harmony in your financial existence.

When you invest all the energy working on debt retirement, you won't have the money available in case of a disaster. Or if you're wasting the whole day today concentrating on the schedule, you can't properly save for retirement.

A money mantra lets you have a financial target at the forefront of your mind, making taking steps simpler to produce the outcomes you like. Now let's take a peek at how to build a great personal finance mantra.

A MONEY MANTRA

A money motto is a clear statement of what you intend to do in your financial existence. This can either push you to make financially good decisions or discourage you from making poor ones. Its function is to remind you and give you assurance in your everyday life. You state what you wish to manifest, and you are encouraged to behave through the act of having the idea in mind. Start by dreaming about a particular financial target you would like to accomplish during the next six months.

THE DEBT SNOWBALL METHOD

The debt snowball approach is a debt management technique where you pay off debt in proportion from smallest to highest, gathering traction when each balance is taken out. Once the smallest loan is taken off in full, the interest you owe on the loan will be transferred into the next smallest balance.

It works as mentioned below:

Step I

List your debts from smallest to largest regardless of the interest rate.

Step II

Minimum payments should be made on your all debts besides the smallest ones.

Step III

Pay as much as possible on the smallest debt of yours.

Step IV

Repeat until each debt is paid in full.

Illustration of the Debt Snowball

Suppose you have four debts:

$500 medical bill—$50 payment

$2,500 credit card debt—$63 payment

$7,000 car loan—$135 payment

$10,000 student loan—$96 payment

Following the form of debt reduction, you will be paying small contributions on anything but the hospital bill. But let's imagine you get an additional $500 a month because you've taken a side work to cut back your costs to the absolute minimum. If you spend it on the hospital bill $550 a month (the cost of $50 plus the remaining $500), the interest will go free in one month. You would then take the $550 freed-up next month to strike the credit card balance, charging $613 in sum ($550 plus the minimum amount of $63). This way you'll say goodbye to your credit card in just four months. You make it pay off!

Now hit the auto loan to the amount of $748 a month in the nose. It'll head off into the sunset within 10 months. You are all on track! You will add $844 a month against it by *the* time you hit the student loan — which is the main liability. That means that it will be also paid in just about 12 months. Today 's choices that you make will affect tomorrow. And make yourself wise.

CHAPTER 8:

Can I raise My Score to 800+ Points?

Now it is time for the hard part. Maybe you have been doing some of the work that we go through in this guidebook, and you have seen a nice increase in the amount of your FICO score.

This is always good news, but now we want to see further if we can get our score to 800 or higher. Only the elite have this kind of score. It is hard to get it because it requires a perfect balance of credit types, a high credit limit, and no missed payments, among other things. But it is possible.

When you can get your credit to be this high, it is a lot easier for you to go through and actually get credit and loans at any time you would like. If something happens and you have many medical bills to deal with, then this credit score can help you take care of that. It can also be used for non-emergencies as well like if you would like to start a business, get a new house, or do something else along the same lines.

So, how do you make sure that you are able to get your credit score up to 800 or higher? The first thing is to know the facts. Once you are able to answer the main question of "What is a perfect credit score?" you will find that it is easier to take on the right steps in order to figure out exactly what you can do to reach the perfect score. First, though, you need to make sure you know where you stand on the FICO scale.

Once a year, you can get a free annual credit report from any of the country's top credit bureaus, all three of them. If you go through this and find any issues on any of them (sometimes a mistake will show up on one and not on the others), then this is the time to fix them. You will never get to an 800+ score if there are a bunch of errors in your report.

The next thing that you can focus on is establishing a long history of credit.

Most of the time, with a few exceptions, lenders are going to view borrowers with short histories of credit as riskier to work with. To reach a credit score that is 800 or higher, you have to establish, and then also maintain a long history. So even if you are not using some of the accounts, keeping them open will help you to get that score up.

As we have mentioned a bit before, you need to make sure that all of your bills are paid on time. There isn't a single person who has an 800+ credit score who also has a missed payment, or a bunch of missed payments, on their report. Paying your bills late or not paying the bills at all is going to decrease your score. If you have trouble remembering the due dates, then consider signing up so for automatic payments and have that taken care of for you.

You also need to take the time to redefine your credit card usage. About 30 percent of the score you have will consist of the utilization rate for your credit, which is going to be the amount of debt you owe divided by the total credit available. Typically, we want to stay under 30 percent, but if you are trying to get a higher score, then staying under 10 percent is best.

One thing that we have not talked about much in this guidebook yet but will help you to get that higher score you want, is to learn how to diversify the accounts that you are holding onto. This is one of the best ways to strengthen your credit, and while it can take some time to accomplish this, you will find it is a great way for us to make sure your credit score is able to go up.

You can make your credit score stronger when you are able to diversify your accounts. This is not an excuse to go out there and open up 10 different card accounts at a time. What it means is that you should have a mix of different types of credit, such as an auto loan, a student loan, a mortgage, and a credit card. Ten credit cards are not going to be a diverse mix of debt or show responsibility with your score. But having a bunch of different accounts, even if some of them have been paid off, is going to be a much better option to work with.

While you work on your credit score, you need to make sure that you cut your spending and create a budget that you are able to stick with. This helps you to stay within means that you can afford and makes it less likely that you are going to fall into trouble with your spending. Although it is true that your credit is not going to factor in your income, living within your means, no matter what that number is, is a great way to raise your score.

Next on the list is to find ways that you can limit the liability that you are dealing with. When you go to co-sign a loan, remember that this may seem like a nice thing to do, but you are really taking on a risk for another person. If you do this for someone who is not able to manage their debt all that well, it is going to negatively affect your score because you will be responsible for that debt as well. If you want to make sure that you can get a credit score that is 800+, and maintain that, then it is a good idea to avoid cosigning at all.

In addition to this, you should make sure that your liability is limited in other manners as well. You should always report cards that have been lost or stolen right away. If you don't do this, then it is likely that you will be liable for any of the purchases that are not authorized at the time. And if you are not able to afford those purchases, then your score is going to be the thing that suffers here.

And finally, you need to make sure that you are restricting the hard inquiries that happen to your report. Whether it is you or another agency or institution who is pulling out the credit report and asking for a copy of it, you are dealing with an inquiry. A soft inquiry can happen on occasion, and it is generally not going to be enough to make any changes to your credit. This soft inquiry is going to happen when one of the following occurs:

You go through and do a check on your own credit report.

You give an employer you may work with in the future permission to go through and check your credit.

You have the financial institutions that you do business with go through and check your credit.

You get a credit card offer that has been preapproved, and that specific company goes through and checks your credit.

While the soft inquiry is not going to do all that much to your credit scores, you do need to be careful about the hard inquiry. This is going to be the one that is able to affect your credit score. This is when a company pulls up your credit report after you apply for a product like a credit card or a mortgage. You want to make sure that you can limit the hard inquiries as much as possible to get the best results with this.

CHAPTER 9:

Steps You Can Take to Improve Your Credit Score by 100+ in 30-60 Days

R ebuilding your credit can sometimes be an excruciatingly slow process, yet you can take a couple of accessible routes that may increase your score in as little as a month or two, as talked about in the accompanying segments.

PAY OFF YOUR LINES OF CREDIT & CREDIT CARDS.

Probably the fastest approach to support a score is to lower your debt use proportion, the distinction between the amounts of revolving credit that is accessible to you and the amount that you're utilizing. One straightforward approach to improve your proportion is to redistribute your debt. In the event that you have a high balance on one card, for instance, you could transfer a portion of the debt to different cards. It's usually better for your scores to have little balances on a number of cards than a big balance on a single card.

UTILIZE YOUR CREDIT CARDS LIGHTLY

A significant difference between your balances and your limits is what the scoring formula likes to see, and it doesn't really care whether you pay off your balances in full each month or carry them from month to month. What makes a difference is the amount of your credit limits you're really utilizing at any point intime. You can support your score by paying off the card in full a couple of days before the deadline closes.

For example, if the bills is usually sent out on the 25th, you can check your balance online about 7 days prior and pay off whatever is owed, plus extra to cover charges that may appear before the 25th.

When the bills are really printed, their balances are pretty close to zero.(In the event that you utilize this method, simply make sure you make a second payment after your announcement shows up if your balance isn't already zero.

That will make sure you don't get damaged with late charges and indeed, that can occur, despite of the fact that you made a payment before the end of the month.)

CONCENTRATE ON CORRECTING THE BIG MISTAKES ON YOUR CREDIT REPORTS

If another person's bankruptcy, collections, or charge-offs are showing up on your report, you will need to work on having those removed.

If an account you closed is reported as open, then again, you'll probably need to correct it. Having an account filed as "closed" on your file can't support your score and will hurt it.

UTILIZE THE BUREAUS' ONLINE DISPUTE PROCESS

Some people say they get faster results when following the online dispute process.

Either way you'll have to make printouts of your correspondence and everything you have sent out.

CHECK WHETHER YOU CAN HAVE YOUR CREDITORS UPDATE POSITIVE ACCOUNTS OR TO REPORT

Not all creditors report to every one of the three bureaus, and some don't report reliably. If you can get a creditor to report an account that is in good standing; however, you may see a quick knock in your score.

LOOK FOR ANY ERRORS ON YOUR CREDIT REPORT

You might wonder what the difference is between a credit score and a credit report. Well, a credit report is a report that contains every piece of data used to determine what your credit score is. That being said, there can be mistakes when calculating your score. It has been known that about 21% of people have errors on a minimum of one of their reports. This means almost a quarter of people with credit scores are suffering from a lower score due to errors.

DISPUTE YOUR ERRORS

When you want to dispute an item, you will have to write to the credit reporting agency, telling them that you want to dispute an item, or more than one item found in your credit report. It is crucial that you include the reason you are disputing.

Once done, your request should be sent in a letter through certified mail. It is also essential to request a return receipt. This ensures that the credit agency in question has received your dispute. Make sure you maintain copies of any letters that you send, as well as the items you attach. Doing this obligates the credit reporting agency to investigate and check if your dispute holds water. This typically happens over 30 days.

ACTIVATE AUTO-PAY ON YOUR CARDS

It does not matter if you make use of an actual calendar stuck to your wall or if you use your smartphone's app to set an alert, you should do whatever you can to be reminded when payments on your credit cards have to be made. Ensure that you pay more than the minimum consistently. When you consider that the most significant determinants of your credit score are your payment history and the size of your debt, it makes sense to pay as much as you possibly can towards your debt.

CHAPTER 10:

How to Build a Credit Score From Scratch?

There are several ways and all of them are effective.

THE FIRST IS TO OPEN A BANK ACCOUNT

Having an account open in itself will not increase your score, but it will give you a starting point to show regular income. After a few months, you can ask your bank (remember to show off your best smile) what services they offer to increase your Credit Score. My bank, for example, offers a mini loan of $ 500 tied up to be returned in 6 months. It means that you deposit $ 500, they re-loan them to you at a favorable rate and when, in 6 months, you finish paying the installments, they give you back the $ 500. Practically in 6 months, you paid interest as a "tax" with the sole purpose of accumulating points. To put it in simpler words: from 500 and 500 you return, then you pay 500 in installments + interest and you return 500 at the end. It is an expense, but this type of loan guarantees you a considerable accumulation of points, but only if you are regular in payments.

THE SECOND IS TO APPLY FOR A SECURED CREDIT CARD

Unlike traditional credit cards, you do not have to show any kind of entry to get approval, but you also have a usage limit. The only thing required is a deposit which is returned to you after a year of regular use. Until a couple of years ago, the deposit was around 200 euros, but with the debt problems that developed after the recession, all the major credit companies have lowered the costs. For example, I applied with Capital One (but there are many others like Discover). The deposit was only $ 49, and the card limit was $ 200 a month with the option of 2% cash back on gas or restaurant expenses. I started using it regularly every month ONLY for these two things and, after a year, my Credit Score was already considered very good, they also returned the deposit and the cash back and the credit limit rose to 500 dollars after only six months. Of course you are not obliged to use it only for these things, but I have limited myself for two reasons.

The first is to accumulate cash back (i.e. a refund) at the end of the year. The second is to make sure I never use more than 30% of the card limit. Which brings me to the next point.

NEVER EXCEED 30% OF THE CREDIT CARD LIMIT

Believe it or not, it is essential that you show that you do not need a credit card to pay for your things, but that you use it only when strictly necessary or as an optional choice.

The more you use it constantly the better, but judiciously.

PAY YOUR INSTALLMENTS REGULARLY

All the above points have absolutely no value if you are not constant in payments. No one here scales your loan or credit card debts from your salary. It is your responsibility to remember when you have to pay or set up an automatic payment from your bank account. I decided to set up automatic payments.

Even if your memory is excellent, you never know what can happen that can distract you and cause you to forget the due date. So I strongly suggest you do the same because even one missed payment will negatively affect your score.

VARY THE TYPES OF DEBT AS MUCH AS YOU CAN

If you can make the Secured Card And the mini loan with the bank at the same time, do it. The more options you have, the faster your Credit Score will grow. Of course, always keep in mind that if you don't pay on time, this will have the exact opposite effect and your credit score will plummet before it even had a chance to grow. So if you're not sure you can do better, don't risk it and wait a little longer.

ADD YOUR NAME TO SOMEONE ELSE'S CREDIT CARD AS AN "AUTHORIZED USER"

If, for example, you are married to an American who has had more time than you to accumulate a decent score (as in my case), it might be a good idea for him to indicate you as an authorized user of his credit cards. This does not mean that you will actually have to use his credit cards, but the more his score improves, the more he will positively influence yours. Be careful though! If you go down, he comes down with you. This type of choice involves a large demonstration of trust so be careful not to betray it.

DOWNLOAD THE FREE CREDIT KARMA APP

Not only does it constantly give you a detailed report of your score, but also what has positively or negatively influenced it, which credit cards or loans are best suited to your situation, your progress, and many other functions. It's all free and, although not updated to the minute, rather accurate. It does not lower your Credit Score and also offers you many other services such as online and free tax returns. Due to Credit Karma, other major credit companies have also had to adjust to offer the Credit Score free check. For example, Capital One and Discover have now integrated this service into their offers (although in a more limited way).

If you follow these tips in a year you can afford to ask for a car loan without having to pay disproportionate interest or even more, depending on your income and your general receivables/payables situation. This reminds me of how important it is to start as soon as possible. Remember that this is the first thing they look at when you need to apply for a loan!

HOW TO GROW A GOOD CREDIT SCORE OVER TIME

Once you've begun to climb your way out a bad credit score, the most important factor then becomes growing your score. Of course, making your payments on time is a great way to balance your previously negative activity, but there are other, more creative ways in which you can achieve this same result.

Let's take a look at the ways in which you can grow your credit in the eyes of a lender.

Negotiate Outstanding Balances

Let's say that you have a debt that ultimately had to go to a collection agency because you refused to pay the debt back within a timely manner. Of course, the debt that you owe is going to reveal itself as a negative on your credit report, but if a collection agency is involved you have the opportunity to change somewhat the way in which this debt is perceived. This requires negotiation skills. By going to the collection agency and negotiating a deal where you only end up paying a portion of your debt instead of the full amount, you look responsible. Additionally, your credit report will show that your outstanding debt has been settled, and this will help to improve your score. Other tips include making sure to put the agreement in writing, stating exactly how much you are agreeing to pay.

Pay Your Bills Twice Per Month

Let's say that you've had a particularly grueling month in terms of unanticipated bills and expenses. To compensate for this, you've decided to spend close to your credit limit. Your credit limit is four thousand dollars, and this month you have already spent three thousand. This situation is not the worst for you, because you know that you have the funds and are planning to pay off the full amount of your debt by the end of the month. Instead, you should consider making multiple payments throughout the month. This way, you will be able to reduce the amount of debt that the credit card company sees. It will seem more like you simply reallocated your funds in a certain way, instead of making it seem like you are maxing out a card and are having trouble financially. This tactic should especially be considered if you own other credit cards that are close to being maxed out or are maxed out in their entirety.

Increase Your Credit Limit

If you are not in the position to paydown high outstanding balances that exist on your credit cards currently at this time, another good option is to request an increase on your credit limit. Especially if you have recently gotten a raise, this could be a great option for you. As we discussed before, having low utilization is key to maintaining a good credit score. By opening up more credit for yourself, it looks like you are using less credit compared to the current credit that is available to you. While this will serve to grow your credit successfully, it can be risky if your spending habits are less than conservative.

You need to make sure that you're not going to immediately spend more of your credit once the credit company has extended it for you. If you have a feeling that this might be a result of a credit extension, seek out one of the other options that were presented in this chapter. Similar to a gambling addiction, sometimes it can seem like spending credit card money creates a thrill because the necessity to pay back the funds is not immediate. If you are finding that you have a hard time resisting the urge to spend large amount of money on your credit card, you might have a credit card addiction. If you notice that you are frequently maxing out your credit card on purchases that are frivolous or unnecessary, you may need to seek help. Even if you don't see yourself as a complete credit card addict, seeking financial counseling might help you save money. Saving money can also help grow your credit score because the money that you save is money that is not being spent in ways in which cannot be paid back. To put it more broadly, learning how to be financially responsible will help you to grow your credit. Knowing what to save and how to save it, as well as learning how to properly manage your funds are techniques that can be aided by hiring a financial advisor.

CHAPTER 11:

How to Improve your Credit Score After Foreclosure and Bankruptcy

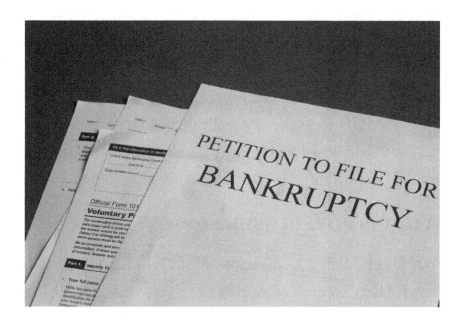

MANAGING FORECLOSURE/ BANKRUPTCY/TAX LIEN AND OTHER JUDGMENTS.

First, what are the public records you can expect on your credit profile? Three kinds of horrible public records used to be displayed on a credit record. But not anymore. You may have heard and wild guesses about this, but straight from the horse's mouth, only one kind of public record is displayed in a credit report: Bankruptcy. But before we jump into that, you need to know that bankruptcy, even though it is the only record displayed on your profile, is not the only one to worry about. Foreclosure is equally crucial. We will start with that, and then we will see how to handle the records on your profile. Here we go:

WHAT IS FORECLOSURE?

Foreclosure is used to describe an official situation where a lender takes control of the asset which was indicated as collateral while applying for a loan. This means foreclosure occurs when a debtor takes over property or assets to sell when the lender doesn't pay back the money borrowed.

Though foreclosure does nothing on your credit profile, you obviously need to avoid it at all costs. Whatever you used as collateral must be something of considerable value to you.

Probably your house (mortgage), your parcels of land, or a vehicle you need for work or family duties. It hurts to see those things go.

Foreclosure is a long and arduous process too. It may span up to 700 days. So, even lenders try to avoid it if they can. Foreclosure usually takes place in different formats. Some are called Judicial, others Non-Judicial. The fundamental difference is that judicial foreclosure requires the lender to obtain official consent from the court before auctioning the property or seizing it. In Non-Judicial cases, the lender is not required to obtain court permissions. They can simply seize their assets.

Just like every other loan, the easiest way to avoid foreclosure is to pay your loans on time.

Now, Bankruptcy?

Bankruptcy is a financial declaration that a person is no longer capable of paying the debts he has acquired. It is a court proven declaration that a debtor has exhausted all means of getting the funds they owed and failed. And now, all creditors will have to be lenient with them. In some way, it sounds like a method of getting relief from your debts, if not all, some.

The introduction of bankruptcy laws came after a long time when lenders could be stigmatized for life, forced into slavery or pash them down to their children.

In our days, when you declared bankruptcy, you are required to declare all of your assets. For example, if you declare bankruptcy with an outstanding of $80,000 you will state all of your personal items and assets from your house, including chairs, dresses, and artwork. It is then the job of the creditor to decide whether some of those items hold value, and can be sold, seized or not. As it turns out, many people often lose more than they were hoping to when they declare bankruptcy, and it becomes a win-win situation for creditors.

Debtors of course realize this before it's too late. This is why many attempt to mess with the records and give false statements or declarations to conceal their assets. These acts are considered Bankruptcy Fraud and are heavily frowned upon in the US. If you are declaring bankruptcy, be set to face the full complications.

Bankruptcy is filed in a situation where a debtor declares that she is entirely incapable of paying further loans. She has tried all other methods, and she is left with no choice than to seek leniency from the court.

When this is approved, the debtor declares the total assets and they are liquidated, in other words, sold to cover whatever it could of the loans. Afterward, the debtor is completely absolved of further payments. The only problem is that it reflects on your credit score for ten consecutive years. This means that every potential creditor can understand that you have been in a financial mess at some point, and you had to give things which do not measure up to the value of the loan. That is never a good sign, and singularly, it will be the reason you might not be able to get a loan for the first years after.

Bankruptcy is declared in situations where a debtor is confident that he could pay the debts but considering his current financial situation, they would need a long period to pay. This time could span into several years. In the end, a repayment plan is approved by the court, and the debtor pays over that period. He is absolved of the debt after payments. Bankruptcy reflects on your credit report for seven years. It faces a lot of criticism, and it could be a reason you're turned down too, but less likely.

Only an organization or individual that is unable to completely honor its financial obligation or make payment to its creditor files for bankruptcy. This goes to say that a bankruptcy filing is a legal course of action taken by a company or person to relieve themselves from debt obligations where all outstanding debt of the company is evaluated and paid from the company's assets. As legal proceeding goes, bankruptcy is carried out to give individuals and businesses freedom from debt they have already incurred and at the same time provide creditors with the opportunity to get their debts paid. It can be said to allow for a fresh start by forgiving debts that cannot be paid and at the same time offering creditors a substantive opportunity to get methods of repayment based on the available assets of a person or business that can be liquidated.

Theoretically, this can mean that the ability to file for bankruptcy can benefit a whole economy by giving businesses and individuals a second chance to have the utmost access to consumer credit and by providing creditors with a reliable measure of debt repayment. Once the bankruptcy proceeding is successfully completed, the debtor is to be relieved of their obligation from the debt that has been incurred before filing for bankruptcy. However, it will be on their credit record that such a person has acquired debts before and filed for bankruptcy. This information is going to remain on the record for about seven to ten years depending on the type of bankruptcy filed.

TYPES OF BANKRUPTCY

There are two types of bankruptcy.

Debt Discharge

This is simply the cancellation of debt, thanks to bankruptcy. Based on the Internal Revenue Code, a debtor must add into their gross income, the discharge of indebtedness after which a court must have discharged his/her debt upon meeting all conditions.

However, if a debtor should refuse financial counseling, commits a crime, fail to fully explain the loss of his/her assets, provide false information during court proceedings or basically disobey the orders of the court, a judge can rightfully refuse to discharge the debt of such a person.

The Payment Plan

This is a kind of bankruptcy filed, where a debtor and his/her lawyer submit to the court, a kind of repayment plan of how the debtor plans to pay off his/her debts in three to five years. This plan is dependent on the debtor's income, food, and utilities, tax, and healthcare expenses.

Should the court approve the plan, the debtor proceeds to make the payments required as stipulated in the plan. If such a debtor is consistent with the payments, the remaining debts at the end of the three to five-year period will be discharged. The payments are made to a trustee from the bankruptcy court that then proceeds to pay the creditors while getting a commission too.

CONCERNING BUSINESS, THE TWO TYPES OF BANKRUPTCY ARE:

Reorganization Bankruptcy

This is a kind of bankruptcy filed which is meant to help business owners who have serious issues with their business but still have regular income and valuable assets, reorganize the business. The business is allowed to continue its operations with the court's supervision of course.

The creditors aren't allowed to interfere with the debtors during the supervision. Business owners will have to share their reorganization plan with the creditors and provide them with part of the payment. But if the creditors do not agree with the plan, they have the right to file a competing plan.

Farming Bankruptcy

It is a type of bankruptcy specially designed for farmers of the same family. It is to help the family reorganize their farming business as well as settle all their debts.

The unpredictable nature of farming and seasonal trends are factors that are seriously considered.

THE BASIC OF CREDIT CARD DEBT AND BANKRUPTCY

People know the basics about credit cards. Once you are approved, you then receive your card and activate it. You can use it for pretty much anything, such as for purchasing groceries, clothing, or for paying bills.

The nice part is that you only have to make the minimum payment every month to keep yourself out of credit card debt. Unfortunately, it is this kind of thinking that often leads people into credit card debt.

Below are some basic points that most people don't realize about credit card debt.

Know when short-term loans make more sense

Sometimes we need to get some cash or find a way to pay a few bills quickly. Many people turn to credit cards for these reasons. They receive their approval within minutes and their card will arrive in the mail in about five to seven business days. However, sometimes it is better to go to your bank and talk to a loan advisor instead. If you need a couple thousand dollars to pay off your medical bills so they aren't sent to a collection agency, it might be best to take out a short-term loan from your local bank or credit union.

Credit card debt can result in bad credit

Paying off your credit cards in a less than a timely manner or missing the minimum payment aren't the only things that are going to result in your having bad credit; having credit cards that hold high balances can also increase your chances of bad credit. This is why it is important never to max out your credit cards. You should make sure you always have at least 30 percent of your credit limit available.

While it is almost impossible in today's world, your best chance of keeping yourself from having bad credit is by remaining as free of debt as you possibly can.

Owing is the easy part, the hard part is paying credit cards back

The reality of life is that you never really know what is going to happen. You could have a job for a couple of decades and then find out that you are randomly laid off due to cutbacks. You could have an illness spike that causes surgery.

There are a lot of situations that can cause you to miss credit card payments and not be able to cover your bills.

You could also find yourself struggling to pay the full minimum balance, so you may decide to pay about half of it every month.

You will find yourself spending more than you make

It doesn't matter how responsible you are with credit cards; one of the biggest reasons people find themselves in credit card debt is because they spend more than they make every month.

Credit cards are very tempting because they provide you with the thought that you can just pay it back later or make smaller payments on the purchase every month.

Although, in reality, you should never spend more than what your monthly income is.

Most people use credit cards to handle emergencies

It is common for people to tell others that a credit card is only used for emergencies, but do you keep in mind what a true emergency is? Most people live paycheck to paycheck. Therefore, when they see their checking account balance drop low and there are several days before their next payday, they will start to think about each purchase they make and wonder if they should use their credit card as it is considered an emergency or a need. The best step for you to take is to start slowly saving a part of your check and place it into an emergency fund account.

People think as long as they make the minimum payment they will be fine

In reality, you always want to make sure you pay more than the minimum payment. Think of it this way: if you have a $75 minimum payment, at least 25 percent of what you pay is going to go toward interest and fees. This means that you are only putting 75 percent of your payment toward paying off your debt. Depending on how you much you owe, this could be a low amount. If you aren't careful, you could find yourself going over your credit limit, which means your credit card company will charge you their over-the-limit fee.

Furthermore, only paying the minimum payment is going to take you years to pay off. It really doesn't matter how low you feel your credit limit is versus how high you believe your minimum monthly payment is. It can still take at least a couple of years to pay off your debt, providing you stop using your credit card.

IMPLICATIONS OF BANKRUPTCY

Before you consider filing for bankruptcy, you first need to understand how it works as well as the pros and cons. It's not a simple issue that can be done quickly but has a complex side only a bankruptcy attorney understands. It would be best if you find out everything you can before filing for bankruptcy. Find below the consequences of filing a bankruptcy.

PROS

Discharge: Getting debts discharged is one major reason people file for bankruptcy. And when such debt is discharged, erasing all your debts as well as preventing creditors from collecting further payments from you, the debtor becomes relieved. It's one huge advantage of filing for bankruptcy. Not everyone who filed for debt discharge is granted. If you owe debts on alimony, tax liabilities or child support, filing for bankruptcy would be a waste of time. Such debts are not forgiven nor discharged.

Automatic Stay: Here is another advantage to be enjoyed when a bankruptcy is filed. It is a situation whereby the person who files for bankruptcy becomes automatically protected from the creditors, as well as the property over the collection of debts. The protection stays until the court finally decrees the debts to be honored and forgiven or discharged. In a situation that involves divorce proceedings, the automatic stay might be lifted.

CONS

Loss of Property: There's a possibility that a bankruptcy filer might lose his property if the court decides it's valuable enough to pay off the debt owed. This would happen if you include your property in your case to the bankruptcy trustee. Your creditor would have higher leverage in trying to get your property especially if you used such property initially as collateral.

Credit Score: Another downside to filing for bankruptcy is that it decreases your credit score. Loaners will only see you as risky when they check your credit history because filing for bankruptcy won't in any way clean up your debt history even though your debt is canceled. However, it's a better option than acquiring debt. You can always rebuild your credit score later.

Privacy: If you're sensitive about your privacy, filing for bankruptcy might not be for you, and this explains why you must do your research if you want to file for bankruptcy.

You can either prepare yourself against the consequences or look for other options. When you file a bankruptcy case, every detail about your financial statements becomes public. In other words, anyone can access your personal information without your permission. The amount you owed, who your creditors were, and your bankruptcy schedule can be assessed easily by anyone. This can be quite a bid deal if you value your privacy.

SO, WHAT CAN YOU DO TO MAINTAIN IT?

Prevention has always been better than cure. But if you are here already, it doesn't help to keep musing over the error you've made. Pick yourself up and be set to make a better impression in future endeavors.

Try to pay other debts promptly. The more you perform better in other debts, the higher your chances of weakening the effects of bankruptcy on your profile.

Building Not Activities Passivity

This may not be explicitly mentioned anywhere, but it is just common sense. Increasing assets increases reliability. If you have sufficient resources, you will be able to mortgage them for credit. So creditors will give you credit for getting a good guarantee in exchange for their risk. Avoid construction liabilities like credit card bills as it will affect your rating negatively.

Keep in touch with credit institutions

Always be truthful about your financial situation and be in good terms with them. Always keep in touch with them and express your inability to pay, if that is the case, and see if it is possible to make an agreement in any way. After all, they want their money and not the rating to fall.

IMPROVE CREDIT SCORES AFTER FORECLOSURE

Foreclosure can drop a consumer's credit scores with a huge margin. If you have had the misfortune of going through a foreclosure, then the following article will tell you how to rebuild your credit score.

A fall in house prices, the subsequent recession, and the high unemployment rate has caused a number of people to default on their mortgage payments. Bankruptcies and foreclosures followed as a result of defaulting on capital and interest on home loans. Since the consumer payment history is one of the most important factors affecting the calculation of credit scores, a foreclosure obviously had a negative impact on the credit rating of all those that lost their houses. Hence, the topic of improving credit scores after the foreclosure has taken on great significance.

A creditor can initiate the foreclosure procedure and complete the entire process outside the court system, assuming that the mortgage deed has a sales clause power. In the absence of a sales clause power, the lender has no choice but to take the borrower to court. In other words, judicial foreclosure is expected. Regardless of the nature of the proceedings, the details are listed in the public record and the consumer's credit report. The information remains firmly positioned in the consumer's credit report for a period of 7 years. As mentioned above, the consumer's credit score decreases from 350 to 400 points following a foreclosure sale.

Although a spotted credit report and a low credit score is a double whammy, a number of creditors give proper credit to the consumer's efforts to improve credit scores. Good credit scores are a must to procure loans at a favorable interest rate, for availing insurance, and for the sake of applying for jobs that require the applicant to assume managerial and financial responsibilities.

Improve post-foreclosure credit score

In order to improve credit scores after foreclosure, you should avail either installment or revolving credit and make it a practice to pay interest on a regular basis. Establishing a history of regular payments can go a long way in helping the consumer build his / her credit scores. The same approach can be adopted by a consumer who is interested in improving credit scores after bankruptcy.

Guaranteed credit cards

People can opt for secured credit cards to rebuild credit since consumers can be approved for these cards within 6 months of a foreclosure sale or discharge failure. These credit cards are guaranteed by a CD which acts as a guarantee for credit card companies. The credit line is usually 50 to 100% of the deposit amount. A practice of repaying the entire balance on the credit card on a monthly basis will result in the credit card company extending further credit lines to the consumer without further deposits as collateral. A secured credit card is converted into an unsecured credit card within 18 months, assuming that the consumer is careful with payments.

FHA secured loans

People whose homes have been foreclosed are required to wait for 3 years from the date of a foreclosure sale to avail themselves of an FHA insured loan. Assuming that the consumer is approved for a secured credit card and brings his / her credit score up to 620 points, FHA secured loans can become the springboard for further improvement in credit scores. The Federal Housing Administration (FHA) offers secured government mortgages that protect the lender in the event that the homeowner's default values on the mortgage. Thus, the consumer can take advantage of a down mortgage by paying only 3.5 percent of the home purchase price.

These measures are not only useful for consumers who are interested in improving credit scores after foreclosure, but also essential for people who are eager to improve their credit rating after debt settlement since a debt settlement does not completely cancel out information from the consumer credit report. The net result is a good credit report and satisfactory credit scores.

Anytime you apply for one of these services with bad credit, you end up paying a deposit. This makes moving into a new place more expensive because you need deposits for all your bills. Fixing your credit means a higher credit score, which can help you avoid these deposits.

CHAPTER 12:

How Can I increase my Credit Limit?

ENSURE YOUR CREDIT REPORT IS ACCURATE AND FREE OF ERRORS

Irst check your credit reports! We each have three credit reports. These include TransUnion, Equifax, and Experian. Credit reports are not always perfect, and many of them can have errors. Up to 1/5 of people have an error on at least one of their credit reports. There are multiple ways to check your credit score. Under the Fair Credit Reporting Act, you are entitled to one free credit report a year from all three major credit report agencies. Below there is a list of some websites you can use to check your credit for free:

☐ www.creditkarma.com

☐ www.freecreditreport.com

☐ www.experian.com

☐ www.annualcreditreport.com

Some credit card companies even offer a free credit report as well. I have a credit card with Capital One that allows me to check my credit for free since I have an account with them. There are many things to keep an eye one when it comes to your credit accuracy. Here is a list of questions to spot potential errors.

◆ Is all my personal information accurate?

◆ Are all my credit accounts being reported?

◆ Are there any missed or late payments referenced that you actually paid on time?

◆ Are there any accounts or applications that you don't recognize?

Simply be sure to check for the accuracy of the information on your report. Keeping a clean report is key for a great credit score.

PAY DOWN YOUR BALANCES

The amount of money you owe accounts for 30% of your credit report. Paying down your balances will definitely increase your credit score, but it is not something that's going to change it overnight. The key here is to be patient. Most people think that when you pay off a balance that it should boost your score immediately. That is simply not the case. It usually takes around 30 days or longer to see the improvement.

OPEN NEW ACCOUNTS

Now, wildly applying for a bunch of different credit cards is not the strategy here. Make sure that you are in a position to open a new account. Credit Karma is great for this. CK suggests new credit cards you can apply for — based on your current credit score — along with showing you the respective approval odds for acquiring them. With this, you can limit the risks of being denied and hurting your credit even worse, since applying for credit and being denied is a black mark on your credit. If you do get rejected, however, don't fear. This will only slightly decrease your credit score. That is why it's important to be aware of your score, to know if you have a good chance to be approved for a new card or loan. Having more accounts will give your credit report diversity. Which is good! The more types of credit that you show you are responsible with, the higher your score will be. But you must be careful! Be sure to stay on top of all your payments.

INCREASE YOUR CREDIT LIMIT

Usually if you have poor credit, you get whatever you deposit for your credit limit. For instance, if someone applies for a secured credit card and they are approved, there is usually a deposit that is required. How much they pay in as a deposit, such as $300, will be their initial credit limit. After a while, of course, you will want to buy more expensive things. You will not want to have a low limit, because it will be a lot easier to max out the card. Which is a major problem for credit. Apply for an increase in credit after you have been responsible and made all of your payments on time with a current credit card. Below you will find some tips for a credit limit increase.

☛ Pick an existing card you already have for the limit increase.

☛ Do not be greedy, only ask for a reasonable increase to show that you are responsible and understand credit.

☛ Plead your case, but don't seem needy. Apply with confidence if you have been paying on time, utilizing the correct amount of credit, your income has increased, or you've always paid the minimum balance.

☛ Wait for the right time to ask. I would recommend waiting about 4–6 months before asking for a limit increase. In those months, you must be sure you are using your loans responsibly. Credit issuers will usually review accounts every 6 months. In fact, people in good standing will usually get a higher limit increase without even asking.

OPEN A SECURED CREDIT CARD / LOAN

As mentioned above, secured credit cards are great for people trying to build or rebuild their credit. A secured credit card is pretty much the same as a regular credit card. The difference with secured credit cards is that they require a cash collateral deposit, which then becomes the line of credit for the account. If you have had trouble getting approved for an unsecured credit card in the past, then the secured card may be right for you. Secured loans work this way as well. Many banks and credit unions offer these types of loans. They are an excellent tool to build your credit.

DO NOT APPLY FOR TOO MANY THINGS AT ONCE

If you decide to apply for a credit card, wait a good amount of time before applying for another one. Problems can occur if you try to use a lot of credit at once. This can make you seem desperate and in need of a lot of money. Many stores offer in-store credit and will give you a discount for signing up. This can hurt your score if you are not prepared!

These store credits will give you a "hard inquiry" on your credit score, which could negatively impact it if you are not approved. If you get denied, try working on improving your score before applying elsewhere. A good amount of time to space out credit applications would be 3–6 months.

CLEAR UP YOUR COLLECTIONS AND DEROGATORY MARKS

Contact debt collectors to see if they would be willing to stop reporting to the credit agency in exchange for a payment arrangement. Normally, debt collectors will settle for less than the total amount if you speak to them and form an agreement. If you have a lot of damage, it may be hard to recover. But paying down your balances will improve your score. Also, once balances are paid off in full, most credit companies will remove bad marks from your report. Which will increase the chances of you receiving new credit and bringing your score up.

FIX YOUR CREDIT UTILIZATION RATIO

Let's say you have a credit card, and the limit is $10,000 If you were to spend $5,000 on something, that would leave you with a credit utilization of 50%. If you were to spend the entire $10,000 on something, on the other hand, that leaves you with a 100% credit utilization. Get the picture? Many people simply do not realize the importance of staying under the correct ratio. The key figure to remember is **30%**! This is the ideal number to stay under with your credit limits. If your limit is $10,000, only spend up to $3,000. If your limit is $200, do not spend more than $60. Simply multiply your credit limit by 0.3 and you'll find your number. Be sure always to try to stay under that 30% for the best credit score.

These 8 tips will provide you the knowledge that you need to take your life back. Do not delay when making these decisions. Your credit is extremely important, and these 8 tips can help you improve it before you know it!

CHAPTER 13:

Should You Use a Credit Repair Company?

The best way to manage your credit responsibly is to get the right financial education and know what is best for you. This will take some time and require you put in the work to learn how everything works. Yet, since your credit scores are so crucial to dealing with your accounts and setting aside cash, you must know as much as you can regarding the credit bureaus that formulate credit appraisals. To assist you with getting started here are key details regarding TransUnion, Experian and Equifax, the primary credit bureaus of the U.S.:

TransUnion

TransUnion has workplaces nationwide that manage various parts of credit: identity theft, credit management, and other credit issues; and types of credit customers, for example, personal, business, and press inquiries. If you discover errors on your TransUnion credit report, you can call them at 800.916.8800 or visit their site to debate them. If you believe that you are a casualty of identity theft, call them at 800.680.7289 at the earliest opportunity.

Experian

Like other credit bureaus, Experian provides a wide range of various administrations for people, businesses, and the media. Experian is based in Costa Mesa, CA, and has a website. If you discover errors in your report or need to report potential identity theft, this credit bureau makes it harder to find them through a phoneline. Instead, they encourage guests to utilize online forms for questions, identity theft reports, and different issues.

Equifax

Based in Atlanta, GA, Equifax has various departments to help people with multiple types of questions and concerns. Their website is additionally set up to have people utilize online forms to work on errors, report identity theft, and handle different matters. In any case, if somebody believes that their identity has been stolen, the individual in question can, call 888.397.3742 to report it to Equifax. If you detect an error you can also go through their phone line to get someone that can fix it for you.

These are the three credit bureaus in the nation, and they each adopt different strategies to enable people to get in touch with them to pose inquiries or address any issues they might be encountering. Rather than reaching the credit bureaus directly, some people prefer to utilize a credit checking administration to assist them with dealing with their credit and stay on top of their funds. The credit bureaus all have related projects; however, most people prefer to utilize an independent organization to assist them with these issues. That way, they get an impartial perspective on their credit score and a lot more services to manage and improve their credit ratings proactively.

MAKING THE BEST OF CREDIT BUREAUS

It is important to learn that all three credit bureaus have sensitive financial data. However, there is no method to prevent lenders and collection entities from sharing your information with the above companies. You can limit any possible problems associated with the credit bureaus by evaluating your credit reports annually and acting immediately in case you notice some errors. It is also good to monitor your credit cards and other open credit products to ensure that no one is misusing the accounts. If you have a card that you do not often use, sign up for alerts on that card so that you get notified if any transactions happen, and regularly review statements for your active tickets. Next, if you notice any signs of fraud or theft, you can choose to place a credit freeze with the three credit bureaus and be diligent in tracking the activity of your credit card in the future.

HOW THE BUREAUS GET THEIR INFORMATION

To learn how the score gets calculated, first, we need to learn about all the different inputs of your score, aka where the bureaus get their info. You may have many factors that report information to the credit bureaus or none. Credit cards are called revolving accounts or revolving debt by the credit bureaus. Each month payments and balances are reported, as well as any late payments. This means that any cards that have your name on them will also report to all the bureaus. This includes cards that belong to a spouse or parent. If you are an authorized user on the account, it gets reported on your credit no matter what. Many people have their credit ruined by a spouse or parent going into bankruptcy or not paying their credit card bills. If your name is on any credit card that belongs to people that may not pay their bills, ask them to take your name off immediately! Installment loans also report information to the credit bureaus. If you went down to your local Sears and financed a washer/dryer set by putting up a down payment, that is an installment loan. The details of these loans are all reported; the total balance, as well as the timeliness and amounts of your monthly payments. If you have mortgages or student loans, that information does get reported. Total amounts due, total paid so far, and the status of monthly payments is all reported. This information is kept track of and organized in their databases.

Conclusion

Thank you again for purchasing this book! I hope this book was able to help you with your needs and to satisfy your questions regarding credit scores.

Now, you have the information that will help you build better credit and increase your credit score. Some of these strategies may not work for your situation or if you have already been employing them. Hopefully, you found a few new strategies to try and will be able to achieve the status you wish to have in your credit scores.

For those who have suffered a financial setback such as years in arrears or a bankruptcy, it will take time. It takes 10 years for bankruptcy to leave your credit history and no longer affect you, regardless of whether someone provides you with good credit lines until then. It could take 10 years for you to get back up into the 800s if you had a bankruptcy and some will not make it because they are not utilizing credit building options as stated in this book.

Anyone who has not nourished a long history with numerous types of credit may also be having trouble gaining a score above 800. However, you have fewer steps to take to get your credit scores higher. You simply need to be paying attention to the credit types you have, ensuring that you open new accounts, keep old accounts open, and establish a long history with consistent and reliable payments, as well as a small "amount owed" in comparison to your income and credit limits.

It is possible for you to have a decent credit score, or more than decent, if you are willing to work towards it. Utilize family to start to gain new credit lines, if necessary. Make certain that if you are paying for something that uses credit to build your score, by putting the funds in your account, you are going home and paying that purchase off right away. It is only the steady, reliable, and consistent credit history that is going to offer a "great credit" appearance, as well as the higher scores.

Since you have the tools available to you now, there is no better time than to get started right away with building great credit and increasing those scores.

As I have shown throughout this book, even a credit repair with a moderate success can bring you countless benefits. All that matters is that you make the time to try. If you go through this process and clear some issues you only need to repeat it in a few years. You already know what to look for and have some experience in how to think and to approach creditors and credit report agencies. The benefits of credit repairing might reveal themselves over an extended period of time but by carefully doing all the steps described in this book you will eventually clear your credit and increase your chances of you ending up with increased scores on a credit application. It will also help you with finding a job, even though your credit is not entirely repaired. When someone is evaluating your credit report and sees the written statements and all the work you have put in the process, it shows how responsible and diligent you are about your finances and says a lot about who you are.

I hope that this book has not only convinced you about the benefits that come with repairing your credit, but also that it has provided a simple and clear explanation of the steps you have to follow in order to do it successfully. I wanted to make credit repair accessible to everyone and suggest the best approach for a different number of problems. Many people become enthusiastic about credit repairing and when they see the effort involved and the time required on the journey to good credit, they get discouraged and give up. Others give up after the first negative response from a creditor or credit report agency and some even go through with it but stop doing things to improve their credit when they've finished the process and still haven't managed to fix all the negative items. Damage control is just as important as the process itself and, as I have said in the section of the book dedicated to this subject, it has many future benefits. The important thing about the whole process is to stay motivated and continue improving.

So, what is next for you? The next step is to begin applying what you have learned in this eBook in your current situation and working as hard as you can to begin repairing your credit. What have you got to lose? If you merely take a step every day, you are closer to your goal every day than you were before. It's like anything else in life; you get out what you put in. All the best to you!

Established business credit also adds value to the business. Any potential future sale of the business will be greatly benefited when the business has an already established positive business credit profile.

The stronger the profile, and more depth there is in trade lines, the more valuable the business becomes to investors and other parties who might be interested in purchasing the business in the future.

A good business credit profile and score can be built much faster than a business owner can build their personal credit profile. And business credit approvals tend to be higher dollar amounts than business owners see through personal credit approvals.

Credit limits on business credit accounts tend to be higher. It is easier and faster to get approved with multiple credit sources.

And it is easier to get approved for multiple credit cards or credit lines with individual business credit sources than it is with consumer credit approvals.

These are only some of the significant number of benefits that building business credit provides to a business and the business owner. For all these reasons, it is tough for any business to truly be successful without establishing a good business credit profile and score and leveraging that to help the business prosper.

You are now empowered with the knowledge and tools you need to ensure your business can obtain and maintain an excellent business credit profile and score. Put your knowledge to use today and get started on building business credit for your business or using business credit to help you start a new business venture.

Once you have built a positive business credit profile, you can finally have the positive business credit and financial future you deserve.

Made in the USA
Middletown, DE
09 February 2023

24487961R00186